Make Your Own

Convenience Foods

How to Make Chemical-Free Foods That Are Fast, Simple and Economical

DON & JOAN GERMAN

WITH A FOREWORD BY SAMUEL S. EPSTEIN, M.D.

Macmillan Publishing Co., Inc.
NEW YORK

Collier Macmillan Publishers
LONDON

Macmillan Publishing Co., Inc.
866 Third Avenue
New York, N.Y. 10022

Collier Macmillan Canada, Ltd.

Library of Congress Cataloging in Publication Data
German, Donald R
    Make your own convenience foods.
    Includes index.
    1. Cookery.   2. Convenience foods.
I. German, Joan W., joint author.   II. Title.
TX652.G46   1979   641.5'5   79-10478
ISBN 0-02-543050-5
ISBN 0-02-009630-5 pbk.

First Printing 1979

Designed by Jack Meserole

Printed in the United States of America

This book is dedicated with love to our mothers,
Jeanette and Reba, who fed us when we were young.

Contents

Foreword

Food chemicals are the nation's fastest-growing and most profitable industry. From annual sales of $172 million in 1955, the market reached $500 million by 1972, and is expected to expand still further to $750 million by 1980.

One of the main reasons for the recent phenomenal growth of the food chemical industry is the boom in "convenience foods" —expensive frozen and dehydrated foods, such as TV dinners and breakfast cereals. Not content with adding more and more synthetic chemicals to foods, the industry is now beginning to move aggressively in the direction of synthetic foods, such as Pream and Tang, and simulated foods, such as textured vegetable proteins.

In addition to their use as preservatives, food additives are used to replace flavor, color, and texture extracted from natural foods when they are highly processed for the mass market. Just for one class of food additives alone, flavoring agents, it is estimated that there are over 1,100 in common use, over 700 of which are synthetic.

All this wouldn't be too bad if consumers were told what synthetic chemicals are added to their foods and if these chemicals had all been thoroughly tested and shown to be safe. This is, however, far from the case. Present labeling requirements are chaotic in the extreme. So-called standardized foods, such as soda pop, ice cream, and mayonnaise, don't have to be labeled at all. Even in foods that are labeled, the information given is usually uninformative, listing, for example, "certified colors," rather than specific ingredients such as red 40. Furthermore, there are no labeling requirements for possible toxic effects such as "Red 40—Caution: This artificial coloring agent may produce cancer and birth defects."

The Food and Drug Administration (FDA) now regulates all

food additives, with the exception of those directly added to meats, which are handled by the U.S. Department of Agriculture (USDA). Prior to 1958, there were no requirements for the industry to test food additives to see if they were safe. However, in 1958, Congress passed the Food Additive Amendments to the Federal Food, Drug and Cosmetic Act, requiring premarket testing of additives. Exempt from this requirement was a group of over seven hundred commonly used additives, known as Generally Recognized As Safe (GRAS) additives, on the grounds that they had been used for a long time and were therefore considered to be safe. Additionally exempt are those additives that the industry itself considers to be GRAS, although their identity has never been spelled out, and the industry has never been too keen on discussing this.

Additives tested after 1958 and considered to be safe are on the FDA Approved List. If they are found to be harmful, they then go on the Banned List. An intermediate category is the Interim List, for an additive that is found to be harmful but for which the FDA does not consider the evidence to be conclusive and more testing is required. However, the additive can still be used while the testing proceeds. In the case of one additive, red 2, its "interim" status was repeatedly renewed for over ten years, until a reluctant FDA finally banned it in response to strong pressure by consumer groups.

What of the testing? Is it reliable and comprehensive? Can you be assured that there are no risks of getting cancer or birth defects from eating or drinking foods to which profitable food chemicals have been added? The answer, unfortunately, is often *no*. The testing is generally done by commercial testing laboratories or by scientists working in the food chemical industry. Both these groups are, of course, anxious to get information and results that will rapidly clear their product and allow it to be marketed. There is now growing realization, more than borne out by my own personal experience and investigation of industry data, that much of the information on safety is incompetent, biased, manipulated, and even fraudulent. As an example, take red 40, a synthetic coal tar dye and one of the most commonly used coloring agents today, second only to yellow 5. Allied Chemicals, the manufacturer of red

40, contracted to Hazelton Laboratories in 1965 to test this chemical in animals for safety, including tests for cancer and birth defects. The testing done by Hazelton was so bad that a high proportion of the rats in their carcinogenicity test died from pneumonia in the course of the test, making it difficult or impossible to determine reliably whether or not red 40 was carcinogenic. This did not deter Hazelton and Allied from submitting their test data to the FDA, claiming that the chemical was safe. Strangely enough, the FDA accepted this claim in 1970 and registered red 40 for food use. The dye was, however, banned by most other countries. Some later tests have shown red 40 to be carcinogenic; but the FDA continues to allow its use until the tests have been completed.

In congressional hearings before Senator Kennedy in January 1976, the FDA admitted that it had uncovered major evidence of fraud by commercial laboratories testing food additives, besides drugs. The Environmental Protection Agency (EPA) at the same hearings made similar admissions for pesticides. In fact, subsequent EPA investigations have shown that the quality of the data on pesticides, whose residues are commonly found in foods, is so poor that it is very difficult to have any idea at all as to whether or not these are safe.

Most recently, a commercial testing laboratory, Industrial Bio-Test, Northbrook, Illinois, long used by industry for safety testing of drugs, pesticides, industrial chemicals, and food additives, came under suspicion and federal investigation for the quality of its test data. What happened? The laboratory promptly shredded all its records.

To bolster its claims of safety, the industry heavily relies on a stable of academic consultants, often in prestigious universities, such as Harvard. Many of these consultants appear more interested in promoting the interests of the industry than in protecting the consumer. The first question to ask any consultant who assures you of the safety of any product or process is, "Who pays you to say this?"

The incidence of cancer is steadily rising. One in four Americans gets cancer, and one in five of us will die from it. In 1976 there were approximately 375,000 cancer deaths. Independent scientists believe that the majority of cancers are due to environmental pollutants and that these cancers are hence preventable. *One of our major sources of synthetic chemical pollutants is in food.* It is estimated that the average American now consumes as much as five pounds of food additives in a lifetime.

Quite apart from the dangers of synthetic food additives, the nutritional value of convenience and other highly processed foods is low, particularly in minerals, vitamins, and first-class protein. These deficiencies are all the more hazardous because they impact on the most nutritionally vulnerable segments of society, the young and the elderly, who are the highest consumers of convenience foods.

This book tells you in simple and readable language how to reduce your consumption of synthetic chemical additives in food massively, in addition to reducing costs, and how to increase palatability and nutrition. This book should be in every home and library.

—SAMUEL S. EPSTEIN, M.D.
*Professor, Occupational and Environmental Medicine
University of Illinois Medical Center*

Make Your Own Convenience Foods

Chapter 1

Get into a Make-Your-Own-Food Mood

COST. CHEMICALS. CONVENIENCE. These are the main concerns about the food we eat.

You don't need statistics to tell you about cost. Food is expensive and becoming more so. And consumers' boycotts don't work for long because, faced with frustration, shoppers soon give in.

Chemicals scare you, and they should. One thousand Americans die every day—repeat, every *day*—of cancer. Scientists now believe that over 70 percent of human cancers are due to environmental pollutants, including food additives.

Convenience is great. But to get convenience, food manufacturers have sacrificed *quality*. You know things are bad when an eminent nutritionist such as Dr. George M. Briggs, professor in the Department of Nutrition, University of California at Berkeley, says, "The American public is eating a strange diet . . . I wouldn't feed it to my cat or dog."

Why do you put up with it? Face it. You've been conned. You've been told and retold until you believe it that

1. *Costs are up because costs are up at the source.* And they are. But the farmer gets only a small fraction of the cost of food. The prices you pay include a great deal for processing, advertising, packaging, profits, and chemical additives.

2. *Chemicals are necessary to make foods the way you want them.* Fact: Chemical additives are necessary to reduce production costs and increase shelf life. Reputable brands, Breyer's ice cream,

for example, have proven that good products can be made without potentially harmful additives.

3. *Convenience comes in a box of prepackaged food.* You have been sold every timesaving gimmick that electrical appliance manufacturers can devise. And then you are told to eat TV dinners because you haven't the time to cook! It is implied that the big food manufacturers have more know-how and basic intelligence than you do.

COST

There is nothing about home food manufacture that requires great genius. Or, in many cases, elaborate equipment. Nor are the raw materials terribly expensive. When it comes to already prepared foods, however, higher store prices are often due to expensive processing, fancy packaging, costly advertising, spoilage, pilferage—yes, shoplifting adds over $150 per person per year to your cost of living—gimmicky concepts, and phony claims.

Look at a few examples:

· In May 1977, a nine-ounce bag of store-brand potato chips cost 69¢. That figures out to $1.22 per pound for potatoes, which were, at the time, selling for less than 22¢ per pound. The consumer was paying $1.00 per pound for processing and packaging!

· Containers in which our foods and beverages are packaged cost the average family of four almost $400 per year. That's a lot of cardboard and plastic at food prices!

· With clever advertising, the Green Giant Company, for example, marketed boil-in-the-bag vegetables from $3 million worth of sales in 1961 to $18 million worth in just three years to $41 million worth just a few years later. Are these products really convenient enough to justify the extra cost?

CHEMICAL ADDITIVES

Additives are the other thing that should concern you about the food you eat. By common usage, people use the phrase *chemi-*

cal additive to mean something added to the food during processing. Food companies like to confuse you by making all additives sound harmless. Some are harmless, such as ascorbic acid, which is used as a preservative. Ascorbic acid is the chemical name for vitamin C. However, caffeine is added to some foods to enhance flavor. Caffeine is a powerful and undesirable stimulant. Here are some common additives that are natural and harmless:

Additive	Function
Ascorbic acid (vitamin C)	Antioxidant
Lecithin	Emulsifier
Carotene (vitamin A)	Yellow coloring
Vegetable gum	Thickener

On the other hand, here are some that are still authorized for use but considered seriously questionable by many experts:

Additive	Function
BHA (butylated hydroxyanisole)	Antioxidant
BHT (butylated hydroxytoluene)	Antioxidant
Glycerides	Emulsifiers; defoamers
Monosodium glutamate (MSG)	Flavor enhancer
Saccharin	Sweetener
Propylene glycol	Solvent

The list could go on and on. But the question remains: How safe are these chemical additives? And the answer is that no one really knows. Nor does the fact that something is approved by the FDA make it safe. For example:

- Coumarin was used in candy as part of artificial vanilla flavor for *seventy-five years* before it was discovered that it caused liver damage.
- Butter yellow, a widely used food coloring, was a common ingredient in foods for many years before it was proven to cause liver cancer.

- Dulcin, an artificial sweetener that was a forerunner of the ill-famed cyclamate, was used for over fifty years before it was discovered that it caused cancer.

- And jelly beans—fun and yummy! But the FDA recently banned carbon black, the coloring agent used to make licorice jelly beans look black, as well as red 4, which colored some of the red ones. How many millions of kids ate how many billions of possibly dangerous candies?

And not all additives are deliberately added. Some get into our food accidentally, while some occur in nature:

- DDT was hailed as mankind's savior from insect pests after World War II. Now it has been banned because it is carcinogenic—which means it causes cancer. Unfortunately, it is persistent in the very soil in which our food grows, so that we all eat DDT every day, as will our children's children.

- An example of an unintentional additive that occurs in nature is *Aspergillus flavus*, an aflatoxin mold sometimes found on peanuts, wheat, corn, soybeans, rice, and cottonseed. Cooking does not kill this mold. It is believed to be a cause of liver disease, including cancer.

So what is left? Well, young mothers at least can nurse their babies. Or can they?

DDT, as mentioned, is highly persistent. So much so that even after it had been banned for three years, high levels of the stuff were found in the milk of poor black women in Mississippi and Arkansas. PCB, used in manufacturing, is a carcinogen that is being phased out, but was found in amounts as high as 10.6 parts per million in mother's milk samples from ten states. The maximum "safe" level set for many foods is 3 parts per million.

What are we still eating today that is dangerous?

And why must we pay the prices we do for adulterated, refined, nutritionally poor foods that offer the grocer and manufacturer long shelf life and high profits and leave you with less than your money's worth in vitamins, minerals, and the desirable qualities food should have?

It is almost impossible to live any sort of normal life and avoid all unintentional additives such as molds, pesticide residues, and pollution from industrial residues. Theoretically, you could grow a large portion of your own foods; but this is totally impracticable for most people. But by shopping wisely and making your own foods as much as possible you can eliminate or at least drastically reduce those possible harmful additives that have deliberately been added to processed foods.

CONVENIENCE

TV dinners are convenient. So are cake mixes. So are packaged luncheon meats, hamburger extenders, packaged candies, potato chips—the list is as endless as the items in your grocery cart.

But with a little technical know-how and a lot of imagination you can make your own convenience foods—every one of the items listed and more. You can have chemical-free TV dinners that taste great and are really full-sized meals. You can have homemade ready-to-eat cold cereals at substantial savings and with no chemicals and as little sugar as you wish.

SPECIAL DIETS

There are two groups of people in our society who especially suffer from the high cost and low nutritive quality of many convenience foods: the elderly and invalids.

Elderly people, as a rule, require fewer calories than young people, but they have just as high vitamin and mineral requirements as ever. It is a scandal in our society that the price of prepared food sometimes forces the elderly poor to eat pet food (although some dog food may actually be more nutritious than many of the expensive, high-starch or high-sugar convenience foods). Elderly poor people don't need to eat dog food to get good nourishing food at low cost, however. With just a little effort, they can make their own food and enjoy quality for a fraction of the expense of convenience foods.

The poor nutritive quality of foods served in some of our hospitals and other institutions is also a scandal. If you have a friend who is in a hospital or nursing home, ask if his or her doctor will allow you to augment the diet with such nutritious goodies as Appalachian Trail Ration (page 173), homemade yogurt (see pages 59–60), or other foods with high protein and/or roughage content. To be sick or an invalid is bad enough without also having an inadequate diet.

Both elderly people and invalids can find a number of easy-to-prepare, easy-to-digest foods in this book. If a person really has problems, he or she could try some of the recipes in the baby-foods chapter.

MAKE YOUR OWN FOOD

By now you should be in a make-your-own-food mood. If you're tired of paying too much and getting too little when you shop for food, decide right now that you are just as smart as those great folks who bring you Fruit Loops and Hamburger Helper. To get the delicious and nutritious foods your family should and will enjoy—make your own.

Convenience foods are great, but why pay a premium price for them when this book tells you how to make them yourself without chemicals or expensive packaging? So get mad at the big food companies who for years have been telling you, in effect, that you aren't clever or patient enough to turn out better products than they do.

Resolve now to make your own food. And remember this: If you are what you eat, who wants to be a Twinkie?

Chapter 2

Simple Equipment You Will Need

PART of the secret of successfully making your own food is having the proper equipment. Chances are, if you're a typical homemaker, you have all or at least most of the items listed here. If you don't, try to stretch your budget a bit to get them. They'll pay for themselves in a few months.

Here are some of the basic tools you will need to make your own food:

A Blender

This is probably the number-one piece of equipment in the make-your-own-food cook's kitchen. You can use it for the obvious, such as making milk shakes. But you can also use it to

- grind cooked meats
- grind coffee or coffee substitutes
- make peanut butter
- make cheese and meat spreads
- make mayonnaise
- grind herbs and spices
- make baby foods
- make pet foods

Get in the habit of using your blender whenever possible. Make your own bread crumbs with it. Or hamburger extender. Or pancakes. Read the directions that come with it. Learn the tricks of mixing, blending, and grinding. And you'll wonder how you ever cooked without it!

To select a blender, look for two things. First, look for a motor that is heavy-duty and has at least two speeds—you need power for making peanut butter and spreads. Second, choose a model with a container that has a base that unscrews for easy emptying and cleaning.

As food processors have grown in popularity, prices of many blenders have come down, making ownership of this handy appliance more attractive than ever. Some people claim that you don't need a blender if you have a food processor. This is true in preparing selected items, but the two machines complement each other nicely. If you choose to own both, you can get by with a lighter-duty blender, and your food processor can be used for extra-heavy jobs, such as making peanut butter or grinding raw meat for cold cuts.

Keep in mind this all-important difference between blender and food processor techniques: When using a blender, always put in the liquid ingredients first, then add the chunky or dry ingredients. Otherwise, you will get caking around the blades or no blending action at all because large air pockets have been created. When using a food processor, on the other hand, *always* put in the dry or chunky ingredients first, process, then add the liquid ingredients. Otherwise the violent grinding action will spray the liquids all over your kitchen!

A Food Processor

These new devices are so helpful in making your own food that one can pay for itself within a short time. A food processor can be used to perform some of the jobs a blender can do. It can even perform some more easily and efficiently, such as making peanut butter or mayonnaise.

The prices of food processors are dropping fast. A satisfactory model can be purchased for less than $50. But beware: There are two types of machines on the market that are referred to as food processors. One is simply a fancy salad maker/vegetable slicer. Avoid these machines unless you're a real salad freak. The other type is more versatile. You can recognize such a machine when the manufacturer advertises that it will do three things: grind raw meat; grind hard cheese, such as Parmesan or Romano; and knead *bread* dough—that means yeast dough. Even the less useful food processors will knead pastry dough, so read the manufacturer's description carefully.

Follow the manufacturer's directions for using your food processor. Always remember to start with dry or chunky materials, process, then add liquids, otherwise you may have a mess to clean up.

What are the advantages of a food processor? Just consider a few:

- After assembling the ingredients, you can make a loaf of bread, not counting baking time, in about five minutes. Even preparing one loaf at a time (which is all the bowl will hold), that results in five loaves in just about half an hour, with no kneading!

- Unlike a blender, a food processor doesn't develop air bubbles when processing thick foods, such as peanut butter or stiff batters.

- A food processor makes tedious jobs, such as French-slicing string beans and shredding cabbage, fast and easy.

Think ahead when using your food processor, or any appliance. If you use it to make Extended Butter, for example (see page 211), after you've scraped out the bowl, use it to slice vegetables. The butter that remains on the sides of the bowl will be sufficient for preparing the vegetable and it won't be wasted. Or, if you're making a variety of breads, one right after the other, prepare the mildest in flavor first, working up to the strongest in flavor, and you won't have the chore of washing the bowl between mixings.

A Pressure Cooker

If you're looking for convenience and good nutrition, a pressure cooker is the answer. It quickly makes tough meat tender, and it cooks so fast that nutrients aren't destroyed. The fact is that long, slow simmering, as in making soup, does destroy some essential vitamins. But with a pressure cooker your homemade soup takes only minutes to make, yet tastes as though it had been simmered for hours.

A pressure cooker also makes home freezing a snap. And for the working woman or man who must fix a quick meal, it gives the convenience of a slow-cooker and TV dinners combined, plus really tasty food.

Again, read the directions that come with your pressure cooker carefully. Learn all the tricks and safety rules for getting the most out of it.

A Kitchen Scale

How much is enough? A kitchen scale is a handy item when it comes to quickly dividing ground meat into equal-sized patties, putting frozen vegetables into dinner-sized portions, for making wine, and for literally hundreds of other routine jobs.

A Pizza Cutter

Here is convenience for less than a dollar.

A pizza cutter, the type with the sharp wheel that cuts as it rolls, is handy for portioning out pizza. But it's also invaluable for

- slicing noodles into varying widths
- quick-cutting bread sticks
- making square hamburger rolls
- cutting anything that a regular knife might tear

A Meat Thermometer

A good, working meat thermometer is another useful gadget you can buy for very little, often for under a dollar.

Besides the obvious use of measuring the temperature of roasts and hams, a meat thermometer is useful for testing homemade luncheon meats (which frequently contain raw pork) for the adequate internal temperature needed to kill parasites that cause trichinosis.

A Bread Maker

If you're going to be serious about making your own bread, a dough pail with a mixing hook is a real time-saver. They cost from fifteen to twenty-five dollars; if that sounds like a lot, remember that you can save fifty cents or more per loaf of nutritious homemade bread over the cost of expensive commercial "health" loaves.

Some electric mixers come with a dough hook; and this, of course, is very convenient. But for the average family, the pail or pot type with a hand crank is fine. With it, kneading takes a fraction of the time, and standard bread makers handle from four to six loaves at once.

You can also use your bread maker to stir large quantities of other things, such as homemade granola (see pages 49–50), Appalachian Trail Ration (page 173), or nuts for dry-roasting (see page 174).

A Yogurt Maker

If you're really going to get into preparing homemade yogurt— and you should—you'll save about two-thirds of the cost of the commercial variety by buying an electric yogurt maker. Buy the cheapest model you can find.

A Siphon Bottle

Because these are used in old-time movies when one slapstick comedian squirts another, the average cook tends to think of them as toys for heavy drinkers. Not so! After your initial investment of less than fifteen dollars at a good discount store, you can make chemical-free soda pop and sodium-free sparkling water for fifteen to twenty cents a quart. You can also turn homemade white wine into "champagne." You can also keep down the kids' consumption of sugar by making your own sweet drinks.

A Hand Slicer

Not for cutting hands, at least intentionally, this little gadget has a blade mounted on a board or on four legs, over which you can quickly run a potato or cucumber and get uniform slices every time. It costs under two dollars in the gadget section of your department store. For canning, pickling, or snack making, it can save you lots of time.

A *Microwave Oven*

Microwave ovens are becoming extremely popular. And they do save time and energy. But anyone buying one should be sure to get a good model with proper seals and interlocking devices that shut off the oven when the door is opened. These precautions are necessary to avoid the possibility of radiation burns.

Recipes in this book may be cooked in a microwave oven by following the manufacturer's directions.

A *Slow-Cooker*

Slow-cookers offer convenience for families where both spouses work, and they are a good way to cook inexpensive cuts of meat that might otherwise be tough. Meat dishes are not emphasized in this book, but you can get excellent recipes from the manufacturers of the various crockery cookers.

Warning

Appliance manufacturers exercise extreme care in designing and producing the various pieces of kitchen equipment they sell. However, it must always be kept in mind that just about every appliance has some inherent danger *if it is improperly used.* Even a little one-dollar slicer can cut a finger just as easily as it can shred cabbage. And the damage that can come from a misused pressure cooker, blender, or food processor is potentially serious.

So the moral is clear. *Always* read and follow the manufacturer's safety directions *to the letter.* The recipes in this book were all tested within the limits of safety for the appliances used as defined by their respective manufacturers. However, it is possible that other brands may have different safety standards. Check the instructions that came with your own appliance to ensure safe operation.

Chapter 3

Saving Money on Food Costs

Brad is a professional who earns $23,000 a year. He and his nonworking wife have three children, ages ten, seven and four. They have owned their home south of Boston for nine years. Yet Brad senses that something is clearly not right.

"You may not believe this," he says, "but my kids are actually fighting each other at the dinner table for each other's food. They have real skirmishes for scraps, battles which happen in the context of my wife and I thinking we've set out an adequate meal for them."

—Excerpt from "Single Salary Struggle," the *Boston Sunday Globe*, October 15, 1978, by *Globe* staff writer Nathan Cobb

THE COST of food is soaring. Prices of individual items on the store shelves rise constantly, seemingly overnight. And the increases aren't small. Five cents more may not seem like very much, but if an item that previously cost twenty cents now costs twenty-five, that's a 25 percent increase. Multiply that by the dozens of items a family buys each week, and the total increase becomes alarming.

According to the U.S. Department of Agriculture, in July 1978, American families who ate a moderate-cost diet spent the following amounts on food each week

- a young couple, $43.20
- an elderly couple, $38.10
- a family of four with preschool children, $59.70
- a family of four with elementary school children, $72.40

Various factors can affect the amount spent for food. People who live in rural areas may spend less because of a home garden

13

or because they keep a few chickens. As a matter of fact, over 40 percent of American families have a garden of some sort.

Having a teen-aged boy or two can knock the amount spent into a cocked hat. So can feeding a meat-and-potatoes person who insists on steak four nights a week.

However, as a statistical generalization, the lower your family income, the higher the percentage of your spendable income will go for food. The reason is obvious. A millionaire's family simply won't eat that much more than a lower-middle-class family of the same size. Even thinking in terms of eating caviar, there is only so much that people can consume.

Let's compare food purchased by a typical housewife to that bought by a smart homemaker who makes her own food. The items that end up in their refrigerators will be similar, except that the homemade ones will have no deliberately added chemicals and may even taste better and have higher nutritive values. The following comparison is based on cost alone.

These items were not chosen to prove the point that making it yourself is cheaper. They were selected at random and then used because they are items for which do-it-yourself costs are fairly easy to compute. The prices listed for the convenience foods and for the ingredients used in the make-your-own versions are based on a test shopping done on October 2, 1978, in a popular supermarket in western Massachusetts. Recipes for the make-your-own versions are in this book.

What does all this mean to you and your family? The prices above show that making your own food can save a substantial amount of money. The prices given will change, of course, and rather quickly because we are in a continuing inflationary spiral. True, your income will go up, too, but not as quickly as the prices. If you are on a fixed income, such as a pension, you have an even more serious problem.

If you cannot raise your income dramatically, then an alternative way to cope with inflation is to reduce your expenses. Here's how.

Eliminate junk foods altogether. If you and your family are typical, chances are you're getting an inadequate diet. According

Item	Cost to Convenience Food Shopper	Cost to Make-It-Yourselfer	Amount Saved	Percent-age Saved
Bread (1½-pound loaf, natural)	$ .93	$ .38	$ .55	59%
Butter (1 pound regular versus 1 pound extended)	1.35	.89	.46	34
Cheese spread (1 pound)	1.69	1.51	.18	11
Chip dip (8 ounces, bacon horseradish)	.79	.48	.31	39
Chocolate bar (8 ounces)	.99	.74	.25	25
Cream cheese (8 ounces)	.59	.35	.24	40
French-fried potatoes (1 pound frozen)	.55	.19	.36	65
Granola cereal (1 pound)	1.09	.78	.31	28
Mayonnaise (1 pint)	.81	.58	.23	28
Meat spread (4¾ ounces)	.65	.21	.44	68
Melba toast (5 ounces)	.61	.12	.49	80
Pizza (medium-sized)	1.49	.74	.75	50
Saucepan stuffing mix (6½ ounces)	.75	.22	.53	70
Whipped topping (9 ounces) (aerosol can)	.79	.41	.38	48
Yogurt (8 ounces plain)	.41	.15	.26	63
TOTAL SPENT	$13.49	$7.75		
TOTAL SAVED BY MAKING YOUR OWN			$5.74	
PERCENTAGE SAVED BY MAKING YOUR OWN				43%

to a recent study by the U.S. Department of Agriculture, a full 50 percent of Americans are not eating a good diet, and one in five families is eating an out-and-out poor diet.

Another way to reduce your weekly grocery bills is to eliminate high-cost convenience foods and make your own substitutes. Few food budgets are spent totally on convenience foods. But many families spend at least half of their food dollars on such items. If you made *all* of your own convenience foods, you could drastically reduce your food expenses. Realistically, you probably won't do that. But with just a little preplanning, you could consistently shave 20 to 25 percent from your weekly grocery bills. If you are now spending $50 a week on food, you could cut that cost by $12.50 for an annual saving of $650.

It all boils down to this. If you can save $5, $10, or even $25 a week on food, you will have that much more spendable income left in your pocket. Income *after* taxes! Income that you don't have to look for elsewhere.

Making your own food makes a lot of sense from the standpoint of improving nutrition and reducing the intake of chemical additives. And it puts money in your pocket as well!

ENERGY COSTS

In case you hadn't noticed, food is not the only commodity that is getting more expensive. The gas and electricity with which you cook, the electricity that powers your kitchen appliances, the oil or gas that heats the water for washup—all cost more every year.

Making your own food needn't mean using more expensive energy. In fact, saving energy in the form of gas and electricity also usually means saving energy in the form of sweat of the brow. The following tips may really pay off for you in both extra minutes of leisure and extra dollars to enjoy.

- Cook as many things at once in your oven as possible. If you're roasting beef, that's a good time to cook a few meat loaves for luncheon meat, to bake a casserole that can be heated later, or even to roast nuts. Think ahead before you turn on your oven.

- If you really can't efficiently use a large oven, use a small table-top model. The saving in electricity is enormous.

- When using the oven, don't keep opening the door. Each time you do, the temperature drops, and you have to waste energy heating it up again.

- In cases in which the dish you're preparing does not require a constant temperature, turn off the oven and let the residual heat finish the cooking. If a casserole has ten minutes to go, for example, and the heat is up to 300 degrees, or whatever, turn off the oven and let the heat already present finish the job. And when you take the dish from the oven, use the last of the warmth to heat rolls or warm plates.

- Use a pressure cooker for stove-top cooking whenever possible.

- Consider microwave cookery as a possible energy-saver.

- When heating water for cooking, start with hot water from the faucet.

- Don't heat excess water. Cooks have a tendency to fill a kettle and bring it to a boil when they need only a small amount of boiling water.

- If you do heat extra water, use it. For example, hot water not needed for tea can be used to make homemade gelatin desserts.

- Remember that small pieces of vegetables cook faster than large pieces.

- Try stir frying. It's fast, it preserves nutrients, and the vegetables taste great. In fact, an electric wok uses only 425 watts, a fraction of that needed for a regular burner on an electric stove, and is useful for all kinds of cooking in addition to the traditional Chinese dishes.

- Cook at the lowest heat setting that will do the job.

- Thaw frozen vegetables and meat before cooking, unless directions say that the items should be cooked frozen. This will save a lot of energy used for thawing.

- Store hot drinks in a thermos. They taste better than when reheated, and it saves energy.

- Use a small one-cup heater or immersion coil for making one cup of beverage instead of turning on the big kitchen stove.
- Don't use energy-wasting appliances, such as electric can openers, knife sharpeners, or slicing machines.
- Set the butter-softener section in your refrigerator to the "hard" setting; otherwise you are running a heater in your refrigerator to soften your butter!
- In winter chill beverages by putting them in the garage or on a protected porch. But watch out for freezing!
- Get snacks ready ahead of time for the kids. Don't allow them to open the refrigerator and freezer doors constantly.
- Know what you want from the refrigerator or freezer before you open the door. Avoid hunting expeditions.
- In winter, after washing the dishes, let the warm water remain in the sink until it cools. This helps to warm your house instead of the sewer.

Now, how about those appliances you need to prepare food? How much energy do they actually use? For an average household for a one-month period the following usages of electrical appliances are typical:

Appliance	Estimated Kilowatt Hours
Blender	1.2
Broiler	8.3
Coffee maker	8.8
Deep fryer	6.9
Food processor	1.2
Frying pan	15.5
Hot plate	7.5
Mixer	1.1
Oven, self-cleaning	95.5
Range	97.9
Toaster	2.7

The moral is obvious. The little, handy appliances, such as a blender, food processor, or mixer, that make it possible to prepare your own foods use very little energy. The real energy gulpers are your oven and range. And don't forget the self-defrosting refrigerator, which uses 101.4 kilowatt hours of electricity a month. Or the frostless freezer, which uses a whopping 146.7.

To sum up, the place to save energy is with your range, oven, refrigerator, and freezer. And the method is simple:

- Use the most energy-saving cooking utensil for the job at hand.
- Use as little heat as possible.
- Gang up on oven usage.
- Don't open the refrigerator or freezer unnecessarily.

If you want to know just what the kilowatt hours listed in the the preceding chart actually cost, call your electric company or look on your bill. Usually there is a breakdown of charges per kilowatt hour. Just multiply that charge by the kilowatt hours in the chart.

Making your own food can also save a lot of energy. Frozen convenience foods that require long heating in a large, hot oven not only cost a lot per serving, they also cost a lot to cook. Do it yourself, and save in more ways than one!

Chapter 4

Natural "Additives" and Ingredients for Professional Results

IF YOU'VE ever wondered how Kraft gets such a nice, smooth, non-greasy mayonnaise, yet every batch of homemade mayonnaise you've ever tasted is greasy, you've probably concluded that they have a professional secret. And you're right. There is an additive that will make mayonnaise taste better, that will help keep Extended Butter (page 211) firmer longer at room temperature, and that has hundreds of other uses around the kitchen. What's more, this secret ingredient is free. It's water. Right out of the tap.

There are several additives and ingredients that you should know about to make your own chemical-free foods at home and at little cost. You may have to shop a bit to find some of them. But make the effort. It's worth it.

Water

As mentioned, water is a common ingredient in manufactured foods, yet home cooks shy away from using it, except perhaps to boil eggs or to steam vegetables. Recipes for Extended Butter and mayonnaise can be found on pages 211 and 135–137, respectively, but you can also use water

- when making cheese spread, to reduce the calories and the oiliness
- with instant nonfat dry milk as a milk substitute in many cooked dishes

· when you make deviled ham or meat spread in a blender or food processor and you're getting dust instead of spread (Yes, you need a bit of mayonnaise or butter, but if you've added enough and just need moisture, try water. A drop at a time. Look on the cans of meat spread in your market. Water is a listed ingredient in many.)

Water is a "secret" ingredient that you can use to make foods moist, reduce calories, and reduce greasiness.

Lecithin

Lecithin is a food product derived from several sources, the most common of which is soybeans. It is highly nutritious and has the happy attribute of being a natural emulsifier. Don't let that throw you. An emulsifier is nothing more than a substance that lets you mix oil and water into a stable solution. Mayonnaise is an emulsion made with raw eggs (yolks are rich in lecithin), salt, vinegar, water, and oil. Creamy salad dressings are usually emulsions.

Think, for a moment, of the advantages of having a handy emulsifier around the house. When you make butter icing, the butter will mix more smoothly with the milk and have a creamier texture. Fudge won't get greasy on the outside, as it sometimes does. A few drops of lecithin in gravy let you mix any fat you wish to leave in the pan right into the sauce instead of having floating globs of it on top.

Many of the recipes in this book call for lecithin. But lecithin comes in two common types, granular and liquid. For cooking purposes, buy the liquid. It is much more versatile. And a pint jar or can will last for many months, because you seldom use more than a teaspoonful of this brown, thick, sticky, but thoroughly invaluable liquid. Buy it at your health food store.

Tamari Sauce

Tamari is Japanese soy sauce. The kind you get at a good health food store has no chemical additives. It is made of fermented soybeans, water, and salt. Sometimes you can get a variation with mushroom juices in it. But do at least buy the basic tamari sauce. It imparts a meaty flavor to gravies and sauces. It can be used in place of bouillon cubes, gravy mixes, and other flavor enhancers for meat dishes. And if you don't think those you are using need replacing in your diet, just read the list of ingredients on the label.

Incidentally, tamari is not expensive. A quart may cost a bit, but translate that down to the tablespoonful or so you use in a dish, and you'll find you're saving quite a lot over the standard flavorings.

Instant Nonfat Dry Milk

If you haven't discovered instant nonfat dry milk yet, now is the time. The big food companies have, and now you're their competition!

Here are a few uses:

- As a sweetener. Powdered milk is rich in lactose, or milk sugar, which, unlike refined sugar, is good for you. Sprinkle a tablespoon or two of powdered milk on your morning cereal, homemade of course, add regular milk, stir, and you have a smooth, creamy, and just-sweet-enough breakfast dish.

- As a mix ingredient. In making your own fix-ahead items such as biscuit mix or pancake mix, use powdered milk. You save money and add convenience because all it takes is water to make the mix complete.

- In place of regular milk. If you don't like the taste of powdered milk to drink but you want to save money, use it in bread making, in casseroles, or wherever its taste will be dominated by other ingredients.

- To stretch regular milk. A mixture of half instant nonfat dry milk, reconstituted with water, and half whole milk tastes pretty good. And this cuts milk bills considerably.

Baking Powder

This is worth a special mention because it's tough to cook without baking powder. But some research indicates that the aluminum salts created as a residue in goods baked with some brands are possibly harmful. So find a brand that uses either cream of tartar or calcium acid phosphate rather than aluminum compounds. Rumford is a good, reliable double-acting baking powder without aluminum compounds. So are Royal, Swansdown, Happy Family, Jewel, and Dr. Price brands.

In some recipes you can get good results by using an acid milk, such as yogurt or buttermilk, and substituting baking soda for part of the baking powder.

Natural Colors

Naturally, you will want to eliminate synthetic coloring agents from your foods. These cosmetic food additives may contain harmful coal tar dyes. But face it, some foods look bland without a drop of color. You can live without blue, green, and purple. Red is a common, natural color and is desirable in certain things you want to be red—strawberry icing, for example, gets a lovely pink hue just from the strawberries themselves. And if you need to cheat a bit, you can always add a few drops of beet juice.

But yellow is a food color many cooks hate to give up. It makes things look richer. A white macaroni and cheese casserole doesn't look as appetizing as a creamy yellow one. Fortunately, there is a natural food additive that imparts a delightful yellow color to most foods and adds substantial amounts of vitamin A at the same time. The additive is carrot oil, rich in carotene; and you can get it in capsules at a good health food store. When you want something to be yellow, just stick a pin in the capsule and squeeze the oil into your recipe. Just be sure there is some other oily substance in the recipe, or the carrot oil will ball up, as any oil will, and give you yellow lumps. If you add a few drops of liquid lecithin, you can be sure your carrot oil will disperse nicely and give a rich color.

Carob

Chocolate contains theobromine, a close chemical cousin of caffeine. Like caffeine, theobromine is an undesirable stimulant. However, nature has provided a substitute for chocolate. It is called carob, and it comes from the fruit of the carob tree, which grows in the Middle East.

According to legend, when John the Baptist wandered in the desert for long periods of time, the fruit of the carob tree sustained him. The ancients considered it so valuable that they used the seeds of the tree to set the weight of precious stones, hence our modern word *carat*.

Carob, unlike chocolate, is nutritious. And like chocolate, it is delicious. You can buy it in many stores. Some health food stores sell it in bulk very inexpensively.

Unlike chocolate, carob has no natural oil, hence it is less fattening. It is naturally sweet, however, but with healthful, low-calorie fructose or fruit sugar. Buy the toasted variety for a rich, chocolaty taste. And don't forget, to get the chocolaty taste you like, add a few drops of pure vanilla extract to any dish you flavor with carob.

Vanilla

Vanillin is artificial vanilla. It is cheap. It is made from chemicals. Buy pure vanilla extract. It costs more, but you use less.

Cornstarch

Cornstarch is similar to white wheat flour in that the nutrients have been milled out. However, it contains no harmful chemicals and makes a great thickener whenever one is required. Cornstarch mixed with carob and sugar makes a Carob Pudding (page 148) that is a treat the kids will love.

Cornstarch is a safe "additive" and helps give professional results.

Vegetable Oils

Read the label on your oil bottle. If it says "preserved with BHA, BHT," or whatever, make your own choices. If you opt for natural oil, shop carefully and you can find brands with no chemicals. Corn oil keeps well without chemicals, so a few additive-free brands are available. There are also additive-free brands of mixed oils, olive oil, olive and vegetable oil, and peanut oil. Again shop carefully. If everyone supports those firms that make chemical-free products, maybe the other companies will get the message!

Herbs and Spices

Some of the interesting taste in processed foods comes from chemicals. Some comes from herbs and spices. Kentucky Fried Chicken, after all, advertises that its popular flavor comes from "11 herbs and spices."

By learning to use these ingredients you can enhance the flavor of the food you make yourself. Shop for natural herbs and spices, packed without chemicals. And remember that fresh herbs have more flavor and vitamins than dried.

Absolute essentials for any make-your-own-food cook are garlic and garlic powder, onion powder, thyme, basil, oregano, marjoram, dried celery leaves, celery seeds, mustard seeds and dry mustard, Tabasco sauce, pepper, and paprika.

Gelatin

Plain gelatin, available in bulk or in premeasured packets, is an extremely handy and totally natural additive. Although it is not a complete protein, gelatin nicely complements other proteins in any dish in which it is included. In addition to using it for making homemade gelatin desserts, it is a helpful additive in making luncheon meats, mousses, and other dishes where a degree of firmness is desired. Of course, gelatin can only be used in things that will be served cold because heat will liquify it. In general, one tablespoon or one small packet will firm one pint of liquid to the consistency of commercial gelatin desserts. For fluffier dishes, such as mousses, proportionately less should be used.

Gelatin is also useful as a clearing agent in making homemade wine (see page 193).

THINGS TO AVOID OR CUT DOWN ON

White, refined sugar is fattening, and it fosters tooth decay. It is suspected of being a contributor to atherosclerosis. It robs the body of vitamins and minerals that must be taken for its metabolism. Most raw sugar is little better. And brown sugar, for all intents and purposes, is simply white sugar colored brown. White sugar is an additive you can and should do without. Where you *must* use sugar, as in wine making, where the sugar is converted by the action of the yeast anyway, you may as well use white sugar rather than raw because it is cheaper. Otherwise, consider using honey where sweetening must be used. Or instant nonfat dry milk, which contains lactose, which makes fine icings and candy. Or, if your store has it, buy powdered fructose or fruit sugar. Since it is twice as sweet as refined white sugar, you need less. The same is true for honey, which is rich in fruit sugar.

Salt helps to raise the blood pressure of many people. As with sugar, we are conditioned to eat it in huge quantities. Amazing, but celery sticks actually taste better without salt once your taste buds get used to the idea. You can't and shouldn't eliminate salt, but do switch to iodized sea salt, which contains valuable trace minerals. Or where possible, to granular kelp. Kelp is dried, ground seaweed, filled with vitamins and minerals—and salt. It is a natural flavor enhancer. Best of all, if your doctor thinks it would be beneficial, mix your sea salt half and half with potassium chloride, available in every store as a salt substitute. Sweet 'n Low brand has few chemicals compared to most others. Salt mixed in this way is less harmful and tastes great. Morton's markets a table salt that is already mixed with potassium chloride, which is convenient, though it is not sea salt.

If you cannot buy iodized sea salt, be sure to get the proper amount of iodine in your diet by eating kelp or taking an iodine supplement.

White flour is popular with millers because bugs don't like it much. All of the vital nutrients are milled out of white flour, and a few poor chemical imitations are put back in. The manufacturers call this flour "enriched." Get real enriched flour by buying whole wheat flour. In recipes where whole wheat flour just won't work or where your family won't accept the taste or texture, at least use unbleached white flour. Even then, you can sneak in a bit of raw wheat germ and bran, thereby putting back some of the nutrients yourself.

SHOPPING FOR FOOD

At the present time, our labeling laws are inconsistent, haphazard, and poorly informative. Some additives need not even be listed. Food colors are often not identified specifically, so that you may be getting a coloring agent that is potentially harmful. And labels give no information at all about accidental additives such as pesticide residues.

Nevertheless, *be a label reader!* Avoid brands with synthetic chemical additives. Support brands with natural ingredients. Sometimes you may have to pay a few pennies more. Usually, though, you'll save money when you buy natural foods.

Where possible, buy natural meats. Fresh fish is usually natural. Ask about chicken to be sure it hasn't been fed growth hormones. Try to buy from a local farmer. When it comes to beef and pork, try to buy in bulk from someone who raises it naturally. There are farms only an hour or two away from most cities where such items can be obtained, sometimes at less cost than in the supermarket. The trick is to buy in bulk, freeze your supply, and thus save time and travel expense.

Buy whatever natural products you can in your supermarket. You'll save money and you'll encourage the production of such items.

If you've never shopped in a health food store, now is the time to start. Some stores specialize in vitamins but have a few food products; most of the foods in these stores will be in jars, cans, or boxes and may be expensive. For items such as flour, cereal grains, and even honey, try to find a store that sells these foods in bulk.

Above all, remember your goal—to make your own food. For that you need good, nutritious raw materials.

Chapter 5

Easy-to-Make Breads

FROM the Bible: "Give us this day our daily bread." "I am the Bread of Life."

Bread is so basic to man's needs that it has assumed mystical qualities.

From *Gulliver's Travels*: "Bread is the staff of life."

From *The Rubáiyát of Omar Khayyám*: "A Jug of Wine, a Loaf of Bread—and Thou . . ."

So bread is faith, sustenance, and love. Yet the kind most of us eat is filled with strange chemicals, made with insipid flour, filled with water to weigh down the loaf, and serves only to keep the meat and cheese we put between its slices from making our hands sticky. It has been aptly called "the edible napkin."

If you're tired of serving this dubious product to your family yet fear the routine of allowing to rise, kneading, punching down, allowing to rise, kneading, and so on, you will be glad to know that making homemade bread needn't be that hard. A food processor makes it a snap, or get a dough mixer—a pail with a handle that turns a large dough hook—for under twenty-five dollars at a discount store. If not, don't let the kneading scare you. It's not that difficult. Especially if you follow the methods in this chapter.

YEAST BREADS

The only flour that will make good yeast bread is wheat flour. This is because wheat contains a nutritious protein called gluten.

Gluten is a sticky substance that, when kneaded together, has a consistency that will hold air in little pockets as the bread bakes, giving it a light texture that will allow slicing and avoid crumbling. Where does the air come from? From the action of the yeast on the sugars in the bread mix. The yeast, a friendly bacteria, eats the sugars and gives off two substances, alcohol and carbon dioxide. In wine making, in which you also have the action of yeast on sugar, you collect the alcohol and allow the carbon dioxide to bubble off. In bread making, you cook off the alcohol in baking and capture the carbon dioxide in little gluten bubbles to make your mix of flour, water, milk, sugar, and so on into bread.

GENERAL TIPS

Here are some general tips to remember when you make homemade bread:

- Use good flour. Freshly ground whole wheat is fine. But if your family balks at the unusual texture, use unbleached white flour. Heckers is a good brand. So is King Arthur. You can mix it half and half with whole wheat flour if you like. Or add bran or wheat germ for extra fiber. Remember that the recipes in this book are suggestions. They are not carved in stone. So feel free to experiment.
- If you add bran or wheat germ, you may also wish to add a little gluten (you can buy it at a health food store) to ensure that you get a light loaf that doesn't tear apart.
- Use dry yeast. You can get it without chemicals.
- Lactic acid works with yeast to make a light loaf with an excellent texture without the inconvenience of the usual rising, kneading, punching-down routine. How do you add lactic acid? Fortunately, there are several easy ways. One is to use yogurt, which is rich in lactic acid, instead of milk. Another is to use sourdough starter. And still another is to use buttermilk.
- Because the weather or magic or something works on bread, you will find that you never need exactly the same amount of

flour twice for the same recipe. So be prepared to use more or less than the recipe calls for.

- A food processor makes bread making easy. Success depends on developing the proper technique and using precisely the proper proportion of dry to liquid ingredients. The special Food Processor Bread recipe on page 32 details the technique and gives the proper proportion.

- If you use a dough mixer for making your bread, be sure to crank the handle on the dough hook for at least 5 minutes during the kneading process. Then, after turning the dough out onto your floured board, knead it by hand for just a short time until the proper consistency is achieved, kneading in more flour if necessary.

- Get the *feel* of bread making. One woman said that she knew her bread was kneaded enough when it felt like her earlobe.

- To shape the bread into loaves, roll tightly into an oblong, then fold under and seal down the ends so that you end up with a smooth top.

- Coat your bread pans with a thin film of lecithin pan coating to make sure the bread will come out easily. (See page 214 for directions on how to make this.)

- Bread is done when it sounds hollow on the bottom. When the top is good and brown, turn the pan over and catch the loaf in a clean potholder. Thump the bottom with your finger. If it looks done and sounds hollow, it is done. Put it on a rack to cool. And be sure to serve one warm loaf right away as a special treat!

Here are the recipes that appear in this chapter:

Absolutely Easy Yogurt Bread

In a four-quart bowl or in a dough mixer, put:

  2 cups wrist-warm water   *2 tablespoons honey* OR

  1½ tablespoons dry yeast   *molasses* OR *sugar*

Stir to dissolve. Let sit for 5 minutes. Add:

  1 tablespoon salt   *1 cup plain yogurt*

Mix together thoroughly. Using a heavy spoon, stir in:

  about 7½ cups unbleached white flour

until the forming dough starts to leave the sides of the bowl.

If you use the hand method, now is the time to scrape the dough onto a floured board, table, or, best of all, a dough cloth (about one dollar at your local specialty shop). Dust with flour as needed, and knead for about 5 to 10 minutes, or until the dough feels smooth and satiny and pops back when you poke it with your finger.

Now, here's the beauty of yogurt bread: You don't have to let it rise, punch it down, or anything else. Just take a big knife, cut that huge blob of dough in half, knead each half for a few seconds, and shape it into a loaf. Pop them into loaf pans coated with:

  lecithin pan coating (page 214)

cover with a bit of cloth or waxed paper, let rise in a warm spot until the dough comes to the top of the pan (about 30 minutes), and bake in a preheated 350-degree oven. The loaves will take about 40 minutes to bake. Remove them from the pans immediately, and cool the bread on a wire rack.

Total time from start to finish: about 90 minutes. Total work time: about 15 minutes! And you'll have the best loaves of bread you ever ate. *Makes 2 loaves.*

VARIATIONS   Substitute rye flour for about half of the wheat flour. If you want a light bread, add 2 tablespoons gluten to make up for the fact that rye doesn't contain as much gluten as wheat.

Coat the top of the loaves with egg white and dust with sesame seeds or poppy seeds.

Roll out the dough and cut it into buns or breadsticks, or shape it into fancy rolls. Remember, you have a good basic yeast dough and can do practically anything with it.

A dough mixer can handle larger quantities than a person can by hand. If you use a dough mixer, you can easily make 4 of these loaves at once by doubling the amounts in the recipe.

Food Processor Bread

Would you believe that you can mix a loaf of bread in less than 5 minutes with no kneading, no punching down, and very little mess? It's possible with a food processor that's capable of kneading yeast breads. Here's how.

In a small bowl, put:

½ *cup wrist-warm water*	1 *tablespoon honey* OR
1 *tablespoon dry yeast*	*molasses* OR *sugar*

Stir to dissolve. Let sit for 5 minutes.

Place the steel blade in your food processor. Then put into the container:

3 *cups unbleached white*	1 *tablespoon vegetable*
flour	*oil*
1 *teaspoon salt*	1 *cup plain yogurt*

Process momentarily. Add the yeast mixture through the chute and process until the dough forms a ball. Remove to a floured board and cut the ball into four pieces. Return two of the pieces to your container. Process again until a ball is formed. Remove to the floured board. Repeat with the other two pieces of dough. On the floured board, shape the two dough balls into one loaf. Place in a loaf pan coated with:

lecithin pan coating (page 214)

brush with oil, cover with foil, and let sit in a warm spot until doubled in bulk.

Bake in a preheated 350-degree oven for about 45 minutes or until the bread pulls away from the sides of the pan and gives a hollow sound when you thump the bottom with your fingers. *Makes 1 loaf.*

VARIATIONS   You can easily make any type of bread you like if you stick to these proportions of liquid and dry ingredients. Remember, the yogurt enables you to make the bread with only one rising— the one in the pan. Try these flour mixtures:

1½ cups unbleached white flour	*1 cup whole wheat flour* *½ cup bran*

OR

2½ cups unbleached white flour	*½ cup bran*

OR

2 cups unbleached white flour	*1 cup rye flour* *1 tablespoon caraway seeds*

Yogurt Bran Bread

In a four-quart bowl or dough mixer, put:

1 cup wrist-warm water	*2 tablespoons honey OR*
1½ tablespoons dry yeast	*molasses OR sugar*

Stir to dissolve. Let sit for 5 minutes. Add:

1 tablespoon salt	*2 cups plain yogurt*

Mix together thoroughly. Using a heavy spoon, stir in:

1 *cup bran*	3 *cups unbleached white*
½ *cup gluten*	*flour*
2 *cups whole wheat flour*	

Blend well after adding each ingredient.

Follow the directions for kneading, forming, and rising summarized in the recipe for Absolutely Easy Yogurt Bread (page 31). Bake in a preheated 350-degree oven for 30 minutes, or until done. Remove from the pans and cool on a rack. *Makes 2 loaves.*

VARIATIONS   Use all whole wheat flour instead of part whole wheat and part unbleached white. Or use 1½ cups each rye, whole wheat, and unbleached white flour and add 2 tablespoons caraway seeds.

For a delicious raisin bread, double the amount of honey used and add raisins and ground cinnamon to taste.

If you use a dough mixer and wish to make 4 loaves at once, double the recipe.

Arabic Flat Bread

This is the homemade bread to make when the phone rings and unexpected company is due in an hour.

In a large bowl or dough mixer, put:

2 *cups wrist-warm water*	1 *tablespoon honey* OR
2 *tablespoons dry yeast*	*molasses* OR *sugar*

Stir to dissolve. Let sit for 5 minutes.

Stir in:

about 6 cups unbleached	1 *teaspoon salt*
white flour	

Follow the directions for kneading outlined in Absolutely Easy Yogurt Bread (page 31). Using a large knife, cut the dough into

12 parts. On a floured board, roll each section into a 6- or 7-inch circle with a floured rolling pin. Bake on greased cookie sheets in a preheated 400-degree oven until just brown. Be careful, these flat breads cook fast—10 minutes or so is about right. *Makes 12 flat loaves.*

There are three ways to serve these breads. One is to cut them in half, then carefully open up each half to form a pocket and stuff it with a sandwich filling. Another is to cut them across completely and use the tops and bottoms as slices of bread with a filling between the slices. But you can't go wrong by simply serving them warm along with a tub of Extended Butter (page 211).

VARIATIONS These make excellent herb breads. Just add garlic, onions, and/or herbs to complement your meal.

Quick Soda Bread

Here is a hearty, slightly sweet bread that is fast to make because it contains no yeast, so it doesn't require rising time.

In a large bowl, put:

2 *tablespoons honey*	¼ *cup wrist-warm water*

Mix until dissolved. Sift together:

3 *cups unbleached white flour*	1½ *teaspoons double-acting baking powder*
1 *teaspoon salt*	1 *teaspoon baking soda*

Into the honey and water, mix the dry ingredients along with:

1½ *cups buttermilk OR yogurt*

This is a fairly stiff but moist dough. After it is thoroughly mixed, spoon the dough into a standard loaf pan, well coated with:

lecithin pan coating (page 214)

Let sit for 10 minutes, then bake in a preheated 350-degree oven for 1 hour, or until done. Test for doneness by inserting a toothpick into the center of the loaf. Loaf is done if the toothpick comes out clean. *Makes 1 loaf.*

VARIATIONS   Add ½ cup raisins that have been presoaked in water, or add bits of other presoaked dried fruits. Or add ¼ cup each presoaked raisins and chopped walnuts.

If you have a food processor, you can have this bread oven-ready in just a few minutes. Using the steel blade, place the dry ingredients in the food processor container, process for a moment, then add the buttermilk or yogurt and the honey-water mixture. Process until smooth and well blended. Bake as described above.

English Muffins

To make English muffins, understand only one thing: They are grilled, not baked. So all you need to do is make:

your favorite yeast bread recipe—Absolutely Easy Yogurt Bread (page 31) *is fine.*

But use just a bit of extra sweetening, up to:

¼ *cup honey* OR *molasses* OR *sugar*

Instead of shaping the dough into loaves, however, cut it into easy-to-handle pieces and roll each on a floured board until about ½ inch thick.

Using a cutter (a clean tuna can with top and bottom removed is perfect), cut out circles of dough. Dip the top and bottom of each circle into:

cornmeal

put on a cookie sheet, cover, and place in a warm spot to rise. Continue rolling out dough pieces until all the dough is used, or, for convenience, bake the scraps into a small loaf of bread.

After your cornmeal-coated muffins have doubled in size, remove them with a large spatula and carefully grill them on a medium-hot griddle that has been oiled with:

lecithin pan coating (page 214)

The cooking time will vary depending on the amount of heat, the thickness of the muffins, and the kind of dough used. About 8 to 10 minutes per side is average. *Makes about 2 dozen.*

HINT: Try to use a fairly large griddle because, cooking them one at a time, 2 dozen muffins at 20 minutes each would take 8 hours to cook! For a shortcut, grill each muffin for about 3 minutes per side, then finish them in a preheated 350-degree oven until done —about 15 or 20 minutes. Any muffins that are not used may be sliced, wrapped, and frozen for later use. To serve, just split apart and toast.

VARIATIONS   Add one of the following to taste: bran and honey; currants that have been presoaked in water; broken walnuts, dried apple bits, and ground cinnamon; carob or chocolate bits.

French Bread

Here's a way to get raves easily. Just make:

your favorite bread dough—Absolutely Easy Yogurt Bread (page 31) *is fine.*

But use:

½ cup more flour than usual

so that it will hold its shape without a pan.

Form the dough into long cigar-shaped loaves, about 1 foot long by 3 inches in diameter. Then, using a clean, sharp razor blade—a knife usually isn't sharp enough and will tear the bread—make a slit lengthwise down the top of the loaf or, if you prefer, make several diagonal slits. Put the loaves on a greased cookie sheet far enough apart to allow room for rising, cover with a cloth, place in a warm spot, and allow them to double in size. *The recipe for Absolutely Easy Yogurt Bread will yield 2 loaves of French bread this size.*

Now, here's the secret of the crunchy crust that makes French bread:

Bake in a preheated 350-degree oven in which a pan of water is allowed to steam on a lower rack. About 35 minutes should do the job; just watch until the bread is done. The steaming water should be in a pan without a plastic or wooden handle that might burn or scorch. And be sure you don't allow all of the water to cook away.

Bagels

Make bread dough according to the recipe for Absolutely Easy Yogurt Bread (page 31).

Along with the yogurt, add:

2 *slightly beaten eggs*   ¼ *cup vegetable oil*

Knead the dough as usual, then form it into strips about 10 inches long and ¾ inch thick. Pinch the ends together to make a dough-nut shape.

In the meantime, nearly fill a large kettle or wide saucepan with boiling water. Dissolve:

2 *tablespoons sugar*

in the water, and, as it continues to boil, drop in the formed bagels, a few at a time so that they do not touch. In a few moments, they will rise to the surface. Let them boil just until the tops of the bagels have attained that nice rounded traditional shape, then turn them over and continue to boil until the other sides have attained the same rounded shape—about 5 or 6 minutes.

Place the boiled bagels on a greased cookie sheet and bake in a preheated 350-degree oven until their crusts are crisp and brown, about 25 to 30 minutes. Serve with homemade cream cheese (see page 65) and enjoy! Any bagels that are not used may be sliced, wrapped, and frozen for later use. To serve, just split apart and toast. *Makes about 3 dozen bagels.*

Food Processor Bagels

The easiest way to make truly delicious bagels is with a food processor.

In a small bowl, put:

1 tablespoon dry yeast	*½ cup wrist-warm water*
1 tablespoon sugar	

Stir to dissolve. Let sit for 5 minutes.

Place the steel blade in the processor. In the container, put:

3 cups unbleached white	*1 egg*
flour	*1 tablespoon vegetable oil*
1 teaspoon salt	

Process briefly. Then add:

¾ cup yogurt

Add the yeast mixture and process until the dough forms a ball. Remove to a floured board and cut the ball into four pieces. Return two of these pieces to your container. Process again until a ball is formed. Remove to the floured board. Repeat with the other two pieces of dough. On the floured board, shape the two dough balls into one piece of dough. Divide the dough into 18 pieces of equal size. Roll between your hands into strips about 8 to 10 inches long. Pinch the ends together to make a doughnut shape. Cook according to the directions for Bagels (opposite). *Yields 18 bagels.*

Sourdough Starter

Like yogurt bread, sourdough bread is very easy to make. But it does have a distinctive flavor that some people love yet others could do without.

Sourdough bread requires a "starter." You can buy one at most gourmet or health food stores. Or, if you like, you can make one. A starter is really nothing more than yeast that has been allowed to ferment.

In the old days, people couldn't just run out to the store for a package of yeast. So they made their own. One way was to boil a kettle of potatoes, then let it cool and sit outdoors in the sun all day. Wild yeast in the air would settle on the water and, with the help of the nutrients from the potatoes, begin to grow. The cook would then pour the water into a bowl, add flour, and let this mix work for a day or two. The result would be a fine starter of sourdough, for that is precisely how it smelled—sour. By saving out a bit of the flour-yeast starter for the next batch, the cook would have a ready supply of yeast.

Prospectors all carried their little pots of starter and were thus known as "sourdoughs." Some even drank the awful-smelling brownish liquid that rose to the top of a working batch because it was rich in alcohol. They called this stuff "hooch," a slang term that once referred to all strong liquors.

When you make your sourdough bread, either with a commercial starter or with your own, don't drink off the hooch. Stir it back into the dough for a really great flavor.

To Make a Starter:

In a bowl, put:

1 *cup wrist-warm water*	1 *teaspoon dry yeast*

Stir to dissolve. Then add:

¾ *cup unbleached white flour*

(The bowl should be roomy enough for the mix to bubble up.)

Cover loosely, and set in a warm spot for 2 days. That's all there is to it. You have a starter. The longer you let it sit, the more sour it will become.

To Expand the Starter:

In a large glass or stainless steel mixing bowl, mix together:

2 *cups wrist-warm water*   2½ *cups unbleached white flour*

Add your sourdough starter, all of it. Cover and let sit in a warm spot, at least overnight. What you have done is to expand your starter. After it has worked, stir it well, then scoop out 1 cup of the expanded starter and put it in a covered glass jar in the refrigerator until the next time you make sourdough bread. Save some each time you expand your starter, and it will last forever.

Sourdough White Bread

You can use the expanded starter you made a few days before to make this outstanding bread.

In a large bowl or dough mixer, put:

remaining expanded sour-   2 tablespoons dry yeast
* dough starter* (see above)   *(for extra zip)*
2 *cups wrist-warm milk*   2 *tablespoons honey* OR *molasses* OR *sugar*

Stir to dissolve. Let sit for 5 minutes.

Add:

2 *tablespoons salt*   ¼ *cup vegetable oil*
1 *teaspoon liquid lecithin*

Mix thoroughly. Using a heavy spoon, stir in:

9 *cups unbleached white flour*

Allow the dough to sit for a few minutes, then knead it for 5 minutes either by hand or in your dough mixer. Shape the dough into 4 loaves, place in pans coated with:

lecithin pan coating (page 214)

and allow them to rise, covered, in a warm spot until the dough doubles in size—about 40 minutes. Then bake in a preheated 350-degree oven until done—about 35 minutes. The dough will shrink from the sides of the pan, and it is a characteristic of sourdough bread loaves to split somewhat, so, before baking, help this along by scoring the tops with a clean, sharp razor blade. *Makes 4 loaves.*

VARIATIONS Use all or part whole wheat flour in place of the unbleached white. Or, instead of making the dough into loaves, make all or part of it into breadsticks: Roll out the dough ¼ inch thick and cut it into small strips with a pizza cutter. Place on a greased cookie sheet and allow to rise until double in size. Bake until done, then dry out thoroughly in a warm oven. *Dough for 1 loaf makes approximately 3 dozen 8-inch breadsticks.*

Old-fashioned Sourdough Rye Bread

A few days before you want to make this distinctive rye bread, mix up a batch of starter and expand it, using the directions given on page 40. Or just expand the cup of sourdough starter that you have been storing in the refrigerator. But don't forget to take out and reserve 1 cup for the next time you want to make a sourdough bread. Then . . .

In a large bowl or dough mixer, put:

remaining expanded sour-	2 *tablespoons dry yeast*
dough starter (see page 41)	2 *tablespoons honey* OR
2 *cups wrist-warm milk*	*molasses* OR *sugar*

Stir to dissolve. Let sit for 5 minutes. Add:

2 *tablespoons salt*

Mix thoroughly. Using a heavy spoon, stir in:

2 *cups unbleached white flour*	4 *cups rye flour*
3 *cups whole wheat flour*	3 *tablespoons caraway seeds*

Follow the directions given in the recipe for Sourdough White Bread (page 42) for handling the dough and baking. If you wish, oblong mounds of dough may be baked on cookie sheets coated with:

lecithin pan coating (page 214)

rather than in loaf pans. Score the tops with a clean, sharp razor blade. If you'd like to have a nice hard glaze, brush the tops of the loaves with:

1 *beaten egg*

before baking. *Yields 4 loaves.*

Sourdough Health Bread

Make your sourdough starter a few days ahead of time and expand it, or expand the cup of sourdough starter that you have been storing away, using the directions given on page 41. Reserve 1 cup and use it the next time you make a batch of sourdough bread. Then . . .

In a large bowl or dough mixer, put:

remaining expanded sourdough starter (see page 41)	1½ *tablespoons dry yeast*
1½ *cups wrist-warm water*	2 *tablespoons honey* OR *molasses* OR *sugar*

Stir to dissolve. Let sit for 5 minutes. Add:

1 *cup instant nonfat dry milk*	½ *cup raw wheat germ*
1 *tablespoon granular kelp*	1 *cup bran*
1½ *teaspoons salt*	

Mix thoroughly. Using a heavy spoon, stir in:

7 *cups unbleached white flour*

Follow the directions given in the recipe for Sourdough White Bread (page 42) for handling the dough. Bake in a preheated 350-degree oven for 45 minutes, or until done. *Yields 4 loaves.*

Hot Dog and Hamburger Rolls

How come commercial food packagers don't get together? They always seem to put eight hot dog rolls in one package and ten hot dogs in another. You can solve this problem by making your own rolls for your next cookout.

Simply make:

your favorite bread recipe—Absolutely Easy Yogurt Bread (page 31) *is fine*

For hot dog rolls, buy a set of 5-inch-by-8-inch aluminum foil baking pans at a discount store. On a floured board, roll out the dough 1 inch thick. Then, with a pizza cutter, make a 5-inch-by-6-inch rectangle. Cut this into six 5-inch-by-1-inch pieces. (Cut the rectangle in half the short way, then cut each half into thirds.) Place these strips, not quite touching, into the aluminum foil pans coated with:

lecithin pan coating (page 214)

and let the rolls rise, covered, in a warm spot until doubled in size. Bake in a preheated 350-degree oven for about 30 minutes, or until done. Cool thoroughly. Using a long, sharp knife, cut the *center* of each segment three-fourths of the way through; at the segment line, cut all the way through. The size is perfect for standard hot dogs.

Hamburger rolls are even easier to make. Again, roll out your dough about 1 inch thick. If you prefer round rolls, cut them with a clean tuna can with the top and bottom removed. If you want square rolls—and consider the fact that square hamburgers are easier to shape (just press the meat in folded waxed paper, see page 89)—cut the dough into 3-inch squares with your pizza cutter. Place the rolls on greased cookie sheets, cover, and set in a warm spot to rise until doubled in size. Then bake in a preheated 350-degree oven for about 30 minutes, or until done.

The amount of dough that would yield 1 loaf of bread will yield 1 dozen hot dog or hamburger rolls.

Biscuit Mix

Here's a recipe for make-ahead biscuit mix just like the kind you used to buy in a box at the supermarket. It contains no harmful chemicals, will save you money, and can be used any way the commercial variety can.

In your blender or food processor, put:

4 cups unbleached white flour   *3 tablespoons double-*
⅔ cup instant nonfat dry milk   *acting baking powder*
1 teaspoon salt

Spin these dry ingredients together. Then blend in:

½ cup vegetable oil

Empty into a covered container and store in the refrigerator until needed.

To make the biscuits:

In a bowl, add:

¼ *cup water to each 1 cup Biscuit Mix used*

Roll out the biscuit dough ½ inch thick on a lightly floured board. Cut into biscuits (square ones are faster to make and just as good), and bake on a greased cookie sheet in a preheated 425-degree oven for 10 to 15 minutes. *Yields about 5 cups of mix. Each cup of mix makes about 6 small biscuits.*

Chapter 6

Get-Up-and-Go Cereals and
Other Breakfast Foods

RECENTLY, you've been hearing a lot about fasting. Just plain not eating. Even prestigious popular magazines have touted the idea. And it is true. The body does benefit from a fast. And we get one every night.

This is where the word *breakfast* comes from. It is the first meal after the night's fast, and it is important that it be especially good from a nutritional standpoint.

You've read of the numerous studies proving that children who eat a good breakfast outperform those who don't. But you won't read very many studies that examine the relative performance of kids who start out with high-protein, low-sugar breakfasts as opposed to those who munch on the sugary, processed, additive-filled candy that passes for cereal in our society. You won't read of such studies because the food industry usually pays, either directly or indirectly, for nutritional research, and it doesn't want such studies made. What would happen to its profit picture if the mothers of America discovered that many breakfast cereals are nothing more than a few cents' worth of grain that has been hammered, pounded, exploded, stripped of nutritional value, pumped full of sugar, and then resold for many times its real value? You are paying a lot for a pretty box!

Then there are the other convenience breakfast foods, ranging

47

from frozen "TV" breakfasts through frozen waffles and frozen or packaged pancake mixes and so on. Again, you're paying a lot for a little convenience and dubious nutrition.

Here's how to have real convenience and variety in the breakfasts you feed your family while, at the same time, eliminating potentially harmful chemical additives and assuring sound nutrition: First of all, don't count on getting up early to fix a hearty farm-style breakfast like grandma used to make. Instead, make the recipes in this book *now*, and have a supply of homemade convenience foods on hand that anyone in the family can have ready to eat in minutes.

Second, try to get everyone in the family to understand how important a good breakfast is. This means protein for energy in the form of eggs, milk, or yogurt. And breakfast is also a good time for natural sugar in the form of fruit or juice for quick pep. Check chapter 21, "Beverages That Save You Money," for recipes for nutritious liquid breakfast drinks that are easy to make and form a quick meal in themselves. If you enjoy meat for breakfast, be sure to try the low-cost scrapple recipe on page 93.

Finally, keep in mind the recent findings about dietary fiber. Roughage in the diet, especially in the form of bran, keeps the bowels regular and, according to many experts, dramatically reduces your chances of getting rectal or intestinal cancer, diverticulitis, and many of the other illnesses caused by poor digestion and elimination. So for a real "get-up-and-go" breakfast, include a couple of tablespoons of bran in some tasty form!

You will find the following recipes in this chapter:

Crunchy Granola

Most people are introduced to health foods via crunchy granola. And they love it. So much so that the cereal manufacturers are all now in the granola business, though their products little resemble the original nutritious cereal. Boxed supermarket granola is full of sugar and tastes like oatmeal cookies, which, in fact, it resembles nutritionally. And wow, is it expensive! Make your own, and save your money and your kids' teeth.

The theory of making granola is simple. You moisten raw cereal grains with a water-based substance, coat them with oil, and toast them until all the moisture dries out and the small amount of oil makes them crunchy and tasty. If you leave out the moisture, you will burn them; if you skip the oil, the cereal will be so hard you can't chew it. With this in mind, you can easily create your own granola recipe. As a base, most people use rolled oats. You can buy these and all of the other ingredients at any health food store. Try to shop in a "brown rice" store, where cereal grains are sold loose in bulk. You'll save a lot of money that way.

Here is a good basic granola recipe.

In a large pot, heat just until boiling:

½ cup honey
½ cup water
½ cup vegetable oil

2 teaspoons pure vanilla
  extract
1 teaspoon ground cinnamon

For smoothness, it helps to add:

1 teaspoon liquid lecithin

Into this liquid, quickly and thoroughly stir:

7 cups rolled oats
½ cup broken English walnuts
½ cup raw sunflower seeds
½ cup raw pumpkin seeds

½ cup unsweetened coconut
(optional; unsweetened coconut is sold at most health
food stores)

Stir until all ingredients are moistened, then spread in a large, shallow roasting pan or on cookie sheets and bake in a preheated 250-degree oven. Stir often with a spatula during baking. When no more steam escapes during stirring, your cereal is almost done. Test it by allowing a small amount to cool and then tasting it. DON'T let the cereal burn or overcook. This recipe should take about 1 hour to bake, depending on how thinly the mixture is spread in the pans.

After cooking, add:

raisins OR *other dried fruit to taste (optional)*

DON'T add them before baking, or your raisins will resemble bullets! Store the cooled cereal in a dry, airtight container. *Yields about 2½ pounds.*

VARIATIONS   Use apple juice instead of water. Or add more honey for a sweeter product. When serving, if extra sweetness is desired, add a tablespoon or two of instant nonfat dry milk instead of sugar. The lactose (milk sugar) is sweet without being harmful, and the milk powder adds valuable protein to the cereal while creating a creamier dish. It will dissolve instantly in the liquid milk you pour on the cereal.

Vary your granola recipe any way you wish. For example, raw broken almonds are delicious in it. Or bits of dried apple. Be creative.

Bran Granola

To add bran to your family's diet, just put it into your granola! But don't add bran, wheat germ, or any other thin, flaky substance until the baking is almost complete, or it will overcook.

Stir:

1 to 2 cups bran

into the ingredients in Crunchy Granola (page 49) when the granola has about 20 minutes remaining to cook. The bran will add go-power to your granola! *Makes about 3 pounds.*

Low-Cal Granola

Make according to the directions for Crunchy Granola (page 49), but use less oil and honey. These proportions work well:

¼ *cup honey*
 1 *cup water*
 2 *tablespoons vegetable oil*
 2 *teaspoons pure vanilla*
   extract
 1 *teaspoon liquid lecithin*
 5 *cups rolled oats*

½ *cup broken English*
   walnuts
¼ *cup raw sunflower seeds*
¼ *cup raw pumpkin seeds*
 1 *cup bran*
½ *cup raw wheat germ*
 1 *teaspoon ground cinnamon*

Yields about 2 pounds. Each half-cup serving contains approximately 130 calories.

Delicious Hot Cereal

Remember how lousy grandma's oatmeal was? You'll love this cereal! And on a cool morning, the kids will ask for more.

Grind the following ingredients, one at a time, in your blender or food processor until they are coarsely ground. Then dump each into a large bowl:

2½ *cups rolled oats*
 1 *cup rolled wheat (optional)*
½ *cup raw almonds*

½ *cup raw sunflower seeds*
½ *cup sesame seeds*

Add:

 1 *cup cornmeal*   1 *cup bran*

Mix thoroughly and store in a dry, airtight container. *Yields 7 cups.*

To cook, bring to a boil:

1½ *cups water*

then gradually stir in:

  1 *cup cereal mixture*

Reduce heat and stir constantly. In just a few minutes, when the mixture is completely thickened, it is ready to eat. *This makes 3 small or 2 generous portions,* which should be served with a dab of Extended Butter (page 211) and a dollop of honey. Fantastic!

Frozen French Toast

What can the kids fix for themselves when things are hectic or when you want to sleep in the morning? This is no problem if you have homemade French toast in the freezer.

In a blender or mixing bowl, whip together:

2 *eggs*   *a pinch of salt*
¾ *cup milk*

Pour into a shallow bowl, and dip into the mixture:

  slices of homemade bread

turning once to coat thoroughly. Grill both sides for a few minutes on a greased hot griddle or frying pan until golden brown. Allow to cool. Place on a greased cookie sheet, and freeze for a few hours. This will keep them from sticking together. After they are frozen, put the slices in a plastic bag, keep frozen, and thaw and heat individual slices in your toaster as needed. Serve with Extended Butter (page 211) and honey or maple syrup as desired. *Makes enough to coat 6 slices of bread.*

This is a good way to use up stale bread.

VARIATIONS Add any or all of these ingredients to the basic mix: 1 teaspoon pure vanilla extract, ¼ teaspoon nutmeg, ¼ teaspoon ground cinnamon.

Pancake Mix

If you make this easy-to-fix pancake mix, even the youngest child can whip up a super Sunday breakfast.

In a bowl, mix together:

2 *cups unbleached white flour*   1 *tablespoon salt*
2 *cups whole wheat flour*   6 *tablespoons double-*
2 *cups cornmeal*   *acting baking powder*
4 *cups instant nonfat dry milk*

Mix thoroughly, put in a dry, airtight container, and store. *Makes 10½ cups mix or 7 batches of pancakes.*

When you want to make pancakes, simply put these ingredients in a bowl, blender, or food processor:

2 *beaten eggs*   ½ *cup water (*OR *milk* OR
1 *tablespoon vegetable oil*   *yogurt for extra nutrition)*
                                         1½ *cups Pancake Mix*

Blend quickly and spoon onto a hot, greased griddle, turning once when the underside is lightly browned. This will yield about 10 pancakes.

VARIATIONS   For a different flavor, substitute the following for the first three ingredients in the Pancake Mix:

2 *cups unbleached white flour*   1 *cup buckwheat flour*
3 *cups whole wheat flour*

OR

2 *cups unbleached white flour*   2 *cups uncooked Delicious*
2 *cups whole wheat flour*   *Hot Cereal* (page 51)

For a thinner pancake, add 2 or 3 more tablespoons of water.

Frozen Waffles

Waffles stick to waffle irons. For this reason, they need more oil than pancakes. So for waffles, use:

the recipe for Pancake Mix (page 53)

doubling the oil and adding a little more water, to make a thinner batter.

Bake on an ungreased waffle iron. *Yields 4 large waffles.*

To store for future use, separate the sections, allow them to cool and freeze them on a greased cookie sheet for a few hours. Remove and store, frozen, in a plastic bag. Thawed and heated in the toaster, these waffles make a fast do-it-yourself breakfast for the children to make.

Cornmeal Mush

Cornmeal mush? That's something your great-grandmother used to keep *her* family budget intact! But it can be tasty as well as a low-budget breakfast dish. Here's the way to make a variety rich in natural fiber.

In a bowl, mix together:

2¼ *cups cornmeal*   ½ *cup instant nonfat dry*
 ½ *teaspoon salt*   *milk*
 ½ *cup bran flakes*

In a saucepan, heat to boiling:

2¾ *cups water*

Slowly, while constantly stirring, add the dry mixture to the boiling water. Reduce the heat, but keep stirring for about 5 minutes, or until the mixture thickens. Then spoon it into a well-greased 8-by-

4-by-2½-inch aluminum foil loaf pan. Chill overnight in the refrigerator. For easy unmolding, pull the flexible sides and ends of the pan slightly away from the mush and turn the loaf out onto a plate.

To serve, cut into ½-inch slices and fry them on a hot, greased griddle for several minutes, or until golden brown on both sides. Serve topped with Extended Butter (page 211) and honey or maple syrup, or topped with applesauce or other fruit. If you don't tell the family they're eating mush, they'll ask for more. *Makes 2 pounds or about 16 slices.*

Chapter 7

Yogurt . . . Food from Heaven

You've seen the ads. A wrinkled but healthy-looking old woman is eating from a container of Dannon yogurt. The caption reads, "One of Soviet Georgia's senior citizens thought Dannon was excellent yogurt. She ought to know. She's been eating yogurt for 137 years." This ad and others like it have capitalized on the widespread belief that yogurt is a truly health-building food.

What is yogurt? Basically, yogurt is nothing more than milk that has been inoculated with a strain of friendly bacteria, *Lactobacillus bulgaricus*. Health food enthusiasts ascribe many benefits to yogurt. For one thing, the fermentation process converts lactose, or milk sugar, into lactic acid. This makes yogurt very easy to digest. It also makes yogurt much less likely to spoil than fresh milk. In addition, the friendly bacteria in yogurt have a beneficial effect on the intestines, aiding in digestion and, according to Adelle Davis and other nutritionists, stimulating the natural production of B vitamins within the body.

There is a legend that the first yogurt starter was given to Abraham by an angel as a gift from God. And it proved, of course, to be an invaluable food for the peoples of the Near East and of southeastern Europe. Families from those regions who have emigrated to the United States prized their yogurt cultures, and many wished to start making the nutritious food again after they resettled here. In order to transport a yogurt starter from the old country, a housewife would dip a clean linen handkerchief into yogurt, dry it in the sun, and pack the handkerchief in her suitcase. After reaching her destination, she would merely place the handkerchief in warm milk and begin making her family's traditional yogurt once again.

The Almighty sent Abraham a most useful present indeed. But it took the greed of modern-day food companies to spoil and exploit it! Some food manufacturers have jumped on the popularity of yogurt and have filled it with artificial flavors, colors, thickeners, preservatives, and, above all, sugar, sugar, and more sugar. Naturally, they have also raised the price, so that yogurt is now an expensive item on the consumer's shopping list.

But if Abraham and his wife, Sarah, could make yogurt under the primitive conditions in which they lived, then it should be a snap for you to make in your modern kitchen. And, by making your own, you eliminate all harmful chemicals and excess sweeteners, and get a delicious product at about one-third the supermarket price. Here are the only three items you need:

1. MILK. This must be free of penicillin and other antibiotics often fed to animals, or the culture won't work. To be sure of this, you can

- Heat regular milk almost to boiling for a few minutes, then let it cool. (Hot milk will kill the yogurt bacteria.)
- Use canned evaporated milk—not condensed—which may be either regular or skim.
- Use instant nonfat dry milk.
- Use soy milk.

2. A STARTER. A starter is simply some of the beneficial bacteria needed to convert milk into yogurt. It may be in the form of a fairly expensive powdered starter available at your health food store. Your best bet, however, is just to use part of a container of *plain*, unflavored commercial yogurt of an unpasteurized brand, which you can buy at the supermarket. Dannon, Lacto, or Colombo are fine. Don't attempt to use pasteurized yogurt as a starter because it will not work. The pasteurization process has killed the friendly bacteria that are both beneficial to you when you eat it and needed to start a new batch. Once you begin making your own, you can

start each fresh batch of yogurt with a portion of the batch previously made. You will need to use a fresh commercial starter for every four to five batches.

3. A SOURCE OF HEAT. Bacteria are killed by high temperatures. Yogurt bacteria multiply when the temperature is kept between 110 and 120 degrees. Any higher temperature than that will kill the culture. Some people set the fermenting yogurt inside a gas oven, with the pilot light providing the right amount of heat. Others use a heating pad turned to a low setting. You can even bring the mixture to the proper temperature, pour it into a thermos, and allow it to incubate there. The best method, however, is to buy an inexpensive yogurt maker. This is an electric warming tray, sold with containers, that will keep the mixture at a constant temperature.

Here are some basic facts to remember about yogurt making:

· The faster your yogurt sets, the sweeter it will be. Therefore, use a good, constant source of heat. Also, the more starter you use, the less time it will take to make the final product. So use a generous amount of starter when you scoop it out of your previous batch. Since you will be eating it and are not really wasting it, don't hesitate to use plenty.

· If you like sweet-tasting yogurt, use milk that contains more butterfat. If you prefer the tarter variety, and some people do, use either skim or instant nonfat dry milk.

· To get a quick start on a batch of yogurt, don't put a cold mixture in your yogurt maker. Heat the liquid to wrist-warm first.

YOGURT IN COOKING

Throughout this book, you will find many recipes that call for homemade yogurt. Basically, keep these things in mind:

· You can substitute yogurt in a recipe for buttermilk or sour cream and often for plain milk.

· Yogurt will give you lighter pancakes and waffles, faster-made

bread with a marvelous texture, and in general will improve your baking.
- Yogurt is a fine base for making other homemade, natural convenience foods. Recipes containing yogurt appear in other chapters of this book.

Many people believe that yogurt making sounds mysterious. It isn't. It is this kind of mystery that makes food manufacturers rich. Practice a bit. If necessary, buy an inexpensive yogurt maker. It will quickly pay for itself. And if your family eats yogurt instead of ice cream, they'll be healthier for it!

This chapter contains the following recipes:

Basic Yogurt

Keep in mind that yogurt is nothing but milk, cultured by a specific strain of bacteria. So all you need are milk, the bacteria from a starter, and the right growing conditions.

This is the best all-around yogurt you can make. It contains approximately 200 calories per 8-ounce serving.

Bring water to a boil in a tea kettle.

In a 1-quart Pyrex measuring cup, mix:

1 large and 1 small can evaporated milk (18⅓ ounces total)

Stir in:

½ cup plain yogurt for a starter

Be sure it is fresh! Mix thoroughly.

Add:

boiling water

until the level in the Pyrex cup is 1 quart. This will bring the mixture to the right temperature to start in a yogurt maker. Stir, then
pour it into your chosen container. If you plan to make it in a
thermos, heat it slightly to wrist-warm, or 120 degrees—no hotter!
Makes 1 quart or 4 8-ounce servings.

This yogurt should set within 3 or 4 hours, and it will be sweet
and creamy. The longer you allow it to stay on the heat source, the
more tart it will become, so take it off and refrigerate it as soon as
it sets. You can tell when it is done by gently shaking the container. The mixture should move as a solid mass the consistency of
junket.

Use your yogurt maker according to the manufacturer's directions. If it is an open type, you may get better results by draping
a clean tea towel over the cups as the yogurt sets.

Save some of your fresh yogurt as the starter for the next batch.
And keep your utensils clean. If you lick a spoon, then dip it back
in the mixture, you can insert an undesirable strain of bacteria that
will ruin your mixture. After you get the knack of it, you can make
all sorts of variations. Powdered-milk yogurt, for example, is great
for bread making and pancake mix. Or the basic evaporated-milk
yogurt makes delicious cream cheese. Use your imagination!

Low-Cal Yogurt

Substitute:

evaporated skim milk

for the regular evaporated milk in the basic recipe (page 59) OR

Make reconstituted milk using:

3½ cups warm water, between 110 and 120 degrees the quantity of instant nonfat dry milk specified on the package for making 1 quart	*an extra ⅓ cup instant nonfat dry milk to make the yogurt a bit firmer* *½ cup plain yogurt as a starter*

Stir well. This will take 1 or 2 hours longer to set than the evaporated-milk variety. *Makes 1 quart or 4 8-ounce servings.* Each 8-ounce serving contains 125 calories.

Fruit Yogurt

To make delicious fruit yogurt, simply mix:

1 *cup homemade yogurt*	*diced or mashed fresh or*
½ *teaspoon pure vanilla*	*canned fruit* OR *preserves*
extract	*to taste*

When using unsweetened fruit, add:

1 *teaspoon honey*

Makes one serving.

The cost is a fraction of supermarket yogurt's. And you will also eliminate harmful chemicals and cut down on sweeteners.

Do not attempt to add the fruit, sweetening, or anything else while making the yogurt. Ideally, the fruit should be added to cold yogurt just before it is served.

Vanilla Yogurt

Combine:

1 *cup homemade yogurt* (see	*honey to taste*
pages 59–60)	
1 *teaspoon pure vanilla*	
extract	

Stir and eat. *Makes one serving.*

Great!

Swiss-Style Yogurt

This is the popular creamy yogurt that gets many people started eating this healthful food. The fruit is already mixed through, and the yogurt is custardlike in consistency. Unfortunately, in some of the commercial brands the yogurt has been pasteurized so that the beneficial cultures are dead. All that is left is the distinctive yogurt taste. Making Swiss-style yogurt is easy.

Thaw:

1 10-ounce package frozen fruit

Heat to boiling:

¼ cup juice from the fruit

Put the hot juice into a blender and whip in:

1 envelope unflavored gelatin

After the gelatin has dissolved, briefly blend in:

3 cups plain yogurt   *1 teaspoon pure vanilla*
  the fruit and remaining juice   *extract*

Pour into serving dishes and refrigerate until set, about 3 hours. Serve cold. *Makes 6 servings.*

VARIATIONS This may be made using canned fruit in the same manner as with frozen fruit. Measure from the can:

1¼ cups combined fruit and juice

Proceed as with the frozen fruit.

If you wish to use fresh fruit, simmer together in a covered saucepan:

½ pound berries OR peeled,   *½ cup water*
  sliced apples OR peaches   *honey or sugar to taste*

Cook until done, about 10 minutes. Then proceed as with the frozen fruit.

Experiment with flavor combinations. For example, add ground cinnamon to apple yogurt, and so on.

Yogurt Toppings

- You can use yogurt wherever sour cream is called for. Try it on baked potatoes, on rice, or over stuffed cabbage rolls. Stir in a pinch of salt and a bit of garlic powder, chives, or whichever herbs would complement the food you are serving.

- A dollop of plain yogurt makes a delicious low-calorie topping for many vegetables. Take a small amount of yogurt out of your refrigerator and allow it to reach room temperature. Then serve it over beets, string beans, broccoli, swiss chard, or spinach instead of butter.

- Yogurt mixed half and half with applesauce makes a healthful, hearty topping for pancakes or waffles.

- Honey-sweetened vanilla yogurt makes an excellent topping for fresh fruit, especially strawberries or sliced peaches. Try serving it over shortcake instead of whipped cream.

Chapter 8

Cheese ... Better Than

Grandmother Made

THERE IS an old Arabian legend that the first cheese was made when a merchant traveling across the hot desert put a supply of milk into a pouch made from the stomach of a sheep. The rennet remaining in the lining of the pouch reacted with the milk and caused it to break down into curds and whey. Opening the pouch at dinnertime, the merchant tasted the curds, or cheese, and liked it. And he quenched his thirst with the whey.

A similar legend probably exists in every culture, for no food is more universally popular than cheese. It is very nutritious and provides a good way to preserve the protein, vitamins, and minerals in milk for long periods of time.

But, oh, what modern food manufacturers have done to cheese! Some cheeses are bleached with benzoyl peroxide, which may be mixed with alum, calcium sulfate, and magnesium carbonate. Mold is inhibited, ensuring long shelf life, by adding sorbic acid, potassium sorbate, or sodium sorbate. Artificial coloring is frequently added.

What can you do? You can make your own cheese, naturally! And you can follow these suggestions:

- Don't buy American cheese or whatever you choose to call the pasteurized process food that is so popular. Make your own.

- Don't buy blue cheese bleached with dangerous chemicals. Instead, buy Danish blue, which isn't.

- Don't buy cheese filled with artificial coloring or preservatives. Be a label reader. Kraft, for example, makes an excellent New England–style Colby with no harmful chemicals, and you can get additive-free Cheddars if you shop around.

- Don't buy little jars or cans of cheese foods. Make your own to save money and avoid chemicals.

Try these recipes, which are included in this chapter:

French Cream Cheese

Making French-style cream cheese is the next step to making your own yogurt. Here's what to do:

Place a fairly large colander in your sink. Line it with three thicknesses of cheesecloth. Carefully pour in:

2 cups Basic Yogurt (page 59)

Fold the ends of the cheesecloth over the top of the yogurt and gently place a plate or saucer on top to lightly press it down. Let sit overnight. *Yields 8 to 10 ounces.*

That's all there is to it. The whey will drip into the sink, and in the cheesecloth you will have thick, delicious, spreadable cream cheese that can be made into dips or desserts or eaten on your own homemade bagels or bread. If you prefer to save the whey for use in soup, set the colander in a shallow pan instead of in the sink.

VARIATIONS   Add honey or sugar and a little pure vanilla extract for a great fruit topping. Mix with chives for baked potatoes or other vegetables. Experiment!

Cottage Cheese

Plain old-fashioned Junket-brand rennet tablets may be hard to find in some areas, though many small grocery stores still carry them. Unfortunately, this superior product is rarely a supermarket item. However, your local grocer can order them from Kellogg's. Here's the way to use them to make cottage cheese.

In a small dish, stir until dissolved:

2 *rennet tablets*   2 *tablespoons water*

In a large saucepan or the top of a large double boiler, make concentrated skim milk by mixing together:

4 *cups instant nonfat dry milk*   2 *quarts lukewarm water*

Stir in the dissolved rennet tablets and let sit until the mixture is set, about 2 hours.

After the mixture has set, insert a cooking thermometer and heat the mixture gently over very low heat or over hot water. Stirring frequently to separate the curds from the whey, continue heating until the temperature reaches 110 degrees. To firm the curd, keep the mixture at that temperature for 15 minutes, then pour it through a colander lined with three thicknesses of cheesecloth, discarding the whey and retaining the curds. Gently rinse thoroughly with cold water. This will chill the curds and wash away the unpleasant-tasting whey.

Now, pick up the corners of the cheesecloth and twist gently to squeeze out any liquid remaining in the curds. When reasonably dry, place the curds in a bowl and add:

¼ *cup light cream* OR   1 *teaspoon salt*
   plain yogurt

Mix thoroughly, refrigerate, and serve when chilled. *Makes about 1½ pounds.*

Gee Whiz

To make cheese in a jar that will cause the bridge club to vote you a grand slam of applause, follow these directions.

In your blender, whip:

½ cup water   1 teaspoon liquid lecithin

Gradually add and whip in:

¾ pound room-temperature sharp Cheddar cheese, cut into cubes

If the resulting mixture is too moist, add:

instant nonfat dry milk

until it is just right. Scrape into a pint jar or an attractive serving container. Yields about 1 pound.

Store in the refrigerator and serve it as a spread at room temperature for the best flavor, or use it melted over hot vegetables, as an au gratin sauce for potatoes, or melted and served on toast.

Food processor technique

Gee Whiz is even easier to make in a food processor than in a blender.

Using the steel blade, put into the processor container:

¾ pound room-temperature sharp Cheddar cheese

Process until finely chopped. Through the chute, add:

½ cup water   1 teaspoon liquid lecithin

If the mixture is too thin, add:

instant nonfat dry milk

until the consistency is right.

VARIATIONS   Use Colby instead of Cheddar cheese. Or stir in one of the following:

½ teaspoon garlic powder
½ cup chopped walnuts
1 tablespoon each chopped onion and chopped green pepper

½ cup raw sunflower seeds
2 teaspoons caraway seeds
2 tablespoons finely chopped pimiento

American Cheese

American cheese is the common name for pasteurized process cheese food. It is the ultimate convenience food, at least in the protein category. Commercially, it must contain at least 51 percent natural cheese; the rest may be a mixture of milk, skim milk, or cheese whey. The low-cal varieties contain water—fine for cutting calories, but not at cheese prices.

To make a 2-pound bar of American cheese, you will need the following ingredients:

1½ pounds grated mild Cheddar cheese
1½ cups very hot water

½ cup plus 1 tablespoon instant nonfat dry milk
½ envelope unflavored gelatin (1½ teaspoons)

Because your blender will not handle all of the ingredients at once, make the cheese according to the following directions.

In your blender, put:

½ cup very hot water
3 tablespoons instant nonfat dry milk

½ teaspoon unflavored gelatin

Whip until the gelatin is dissolved. Quickly add to the hot mixture:

½ pound of the grated mild Cheddar cheese

Whip until blended. Pour into an 8-by-4-by-2½-inch loaf pan that has been lined with plastic wrap.

Repeat this process two more times, until all of the ingredients have been used and the loaf pan is filled. Cover the pan with more plastic wrap and chill overnight before unmolding. Keep cold and slice as needed. *Makes 2 pounds.*

Cottage Cheese Spreads

It is really convenient to have an assortment of those little jars of cheese spread in your refrigerator. With a box of crackers, you have instant hors d'oeuvres; or stuff some celery stalks for your relish tray; or spread it on bread for a quick lunchtime sandwich.

Each of the following can be made quickly in your blender.

Blue Cheese Spread

Blend until smooth:

8 ounces cottage cheese   *2 ounces Danish blue cheese*

Scrape into a jar and store in the refrigerator. *Yields 1¼ cups.*

Pineapple Cheese Spread

Blend until smooth:

8 ounces cottage cheese   *½ cup well-drained canned pineapple chunks*

Scrape into a jar and store in the refrigerator. Chill until spreading consistency before serving. *Makes 1½ cups.*

Tangy Egg 'n' Cheese Spread

Blend until smooth:

8 ounces cottage cheese   8 drops Tabasco sauce

2 peeled hard-cooked eggs   ⅛ teaspoon dillweed

1 tablespoon prepared
   mustard

Scrape into a jar and store in the refrigerator. Chill until spreading consistency before serving. *Makes about 1¼ cups.*

Chapter 9

Luncheon Meat . . . The Ultimate Convenience Food

TAKE two pieces of bread, two slices of bologna, some tomato slices, a bit of lettuce, a dab of mayonnaise—and, let's face it, you have a convenient lunch. You also have extremely expensive protein. And if you want to get the cold shakes, read the label on the bologna package.

Just for the record, sodium nitrate and sodium nitrite combine with amines to form nitrosamines. That means they can cause cancer. They make your luncheon meat nice and pink. Another chemical that is approved by the FDA and is used to turn hot dogs and other similar meats pink is sodium acid pyrophosphate. And a slower-acting additive, commonly used for years, is glucono delta lactone. The next time you pass the delicatessen counter at the supermarket, check the color of most of the luncheon meats on display. It is not possible to achieve this rosy glow without the use of chemicals during the curing process.

Still other chemicals used in luncheon meat improve its shelf life and texture and disguise the flavor of poor-quality meat. Many luncheon meats are also packed with meat extenders, such as non-fat dry milk, starches, or cereals. While these ingredients are not harmful, they're costing you as much, ounce for ounce, as the meat with which they're mixed. This, of course, is not the case when you make your own.

So make your own luncheon meat to save money and to

greatly reduce your family's exposure to many dangerous chemical additives.

For the manufacturer, it is convenient to make luncheon meat in the form of rolls or loaves. It ships readily, slices neatly for quick measuring, and looks nice. It is also convenient for the food manufacturer to grind up gristle and bone with otherwise inedible meats and shape it into very appealing, very expensive (pound for pound) loaves or rolls. You are not a food manufacturer. So you don't have to have neat little loaves or rolls. You don't need a fine texture in order to disguise gristle. And you certainly don't need pink-colored luncheon meat with the attendant chemical risk—and that's no baloney!

Included in this chapter are recipes for:

Meat Spread

The easiest form of luncheon meat to make is meat spread. All it takes is a blender, a little liquid to thin the ground meat, something to hold it together, and some interesting spices.

Cover and cook until the meat is thoroughly done:

1 *pound ground beef*	½ *cup water*

Allow to cool.

Place about one-half of the meat in your blender along with one-half of the liquid. Grind away. Then add:

1 *teaspoon tamari sauce*	1 *teaspoon paprika*
½ *teaspoon garlic powder*	1 *teaspoon salt*

Blend. Then slowly blend in about

⅔ cup instant nonfat dry milk

Empty into a bowl. Grind the rest of the meat with the remaining liquid and repeat the measures of flavorings and powdered milk. Put all the ingredients into the bowl, mix thoroughly, chill until spreading consistency, and use as a sandwich spread. *Makes a little over 1 pound.*

Some meats contain more water than others, so you may need more or less of the powdered milk to achieve the proper texture. Experiment. And if you shop for meat bargains, you'll be able to get nutritious and delicious luncheon meat for less than the commercial variety!

VARIATIONS Substitute fresh pork or pork sausage or a combination of pork and beef for the ground beef. Change your spices! Thoroughly drained, coarsely chopped pickles stirred in after blending also make a nice variation. So does finely cubed Cheddar cheese stirred into the spread rather than ground in the blender. Or you can make a delicious liver spread by substituting small cubes of liver for the ground beef.

Luncheon-Meat Loaf

If you like luncheon meat you can slice, meat loaf is the easiest to make and a universal favorite. Here's how.

In a bowl, mix:

2 pounds ground beef

1 pound ground pork

2 eggs

1 cup finely ground bread crumbs OR 1 cup raw wheat germ or bran

2 tablespoons tamari sauce OR

2 tablespoons Worcestershire sauce

2 or 3 dashes of Tabasco sauce

1 teaspoon salt

1 teaspoon garlic powder

1 teaspoon onion powder

If necessary to make the mixture workable, add:

small amount of milk or water

Now, here is the secret for good luncheon-type meat loaf.

Line a loaf pan with a piece of plastic wrap. Use enough wrap so that there is plenty of overhang. Using a wooden or heavy metal spoon, pack the meat loaf mixture into the lined pan. Actually beat the meat loaf with the spoon occasionally so that it is really tightly packed with no air pockets. When the pan is full, invert it carefully onto a rack set in a shallow roasting pan. Remove the loaf pan and the plastic wrap and you should have a perfectly formed, firm meat loaf.

Using a meat thermometer, bake in a preheated 300-degree oven until the internal temperature of the meat reaches 190 degrees. This will take approximately 1 hour. Allow to cool thoroughly, then slice as needed. Store in the refrigerator. *Makes a 3-pound loaf.*

VARIATIONS Use all beef, all pork, or even pork sausage. Vary your spices to suit your taste. You can come up with an almost infinite variety of combinations. For example:

- Cover the loaf with foil while baking if you prefer not to have a brown outer crust.
- Insert peeled whole hard-cooked eggs in the center as you fill the loaf pan. They'll slice prettily along with the meat.
- Add ½ teaspoon each oregano and basil and dust with paprika for an Italian-style loaf.

Pickle Loaf

You can make very tasty luncheon meat at home with a substantial saving in cost and with no strange or sinister-sounding chemicals. This recipe requires a blender. A food processor would make too coarse an end product, and the hot liquid could splash out of the food processor container.

The best method for cooking the meat is in a pressure cooker, but if you don't have one, a large covered frying pan will do nicely.

If you use a pressure cooker, cook for 10 minutes, or, if you use a frying pan, cook until done:

1½ pounds ground beef, broken up	*½ pound ground pork, broken up*
	½ cup water

When done, put into your blender:

the hot cooking water drained from the meat	*1 envelope unflavored gelatin*

Blend until the gelatin is dissolved, then add:

½ teaspoon garlic powder	*1 teaspoon salt*
½ teaspoon onion powder	*¼ teaspoon ground black pepper*
1 tablespoon tamari sauce	

Blend again, and, a bit at a time, add:

the cooked meat

Blend until you have a smooth puree. Then add:

½ cup instant nonfat dry milk

Blend thoroughly. Finally, without turning on the blender, stir in:

¼ cup drained sweet pickle relish

Pour into a greased 8-by-4-by-2½-inch *aluminum foil* loaf pan and chill overnight. For easy unmolding, pull the flexible sides and ends of the pan slightly away from the meat and turn the loaf out onto a plate. Wrap and store in the refrigerator. Slice cold for an excellent sandwich filling or for other cold-meat uses. *Makes about 2¼ pounds.*

Better 'n Bacon

Until the Powers That Be get around to banning sodium nitrate and sodium nitrite from processed meats, more and more wary consumers will eliminate items that contain these chemicals from their diets. Most people can live very nicely without eating a lot of the "embalmed" meats that are on the market; but, let's face it, doing without bacon can hurt. How else can you make a tasty BLT sandwich? And a couple of strips of bacon certainly complement eggs. But many scientists are warning against eating bacon, especially when fried crisp, because the heat produces potentially dangerous chemical changes in the additives in the meat.

So make your own bacon substitute. Tamari sauce, a very useful and natural additive, has a delightfully savory flavor. With it, you can convert ground pork into a homemade product that has a taste remarkably similar to bacon. It will also save you money and it contains no chemicals. The recipe is simple. The technique sounds a bit complicated, but, once you get the hang of it, you'll find it a snap.

In a bowl, thoroughly mix together:

1 pound ground pork   *1 teaspoon sugar*
¼ cup tamari sauce

Now, tear from the roll 4 sheets of wax paper, each 15 inches long. Using one sheet, make a fold 6 inches up from the bottom. Divide the pork mixture into 4 equal amounts. In the center of the pouch you have formed, place one-quarter of the pork mixture. Next, make a fold in the waxed paper 3 inches down from the top so that it overlaps the fold from the bottom. Then, make a fold 2 inches in from each side. You now have a 6-by-7¾-inch waxed-paper envelope with the pork mixture inside. Turn the whole thing over on a flat surface so that all of the waxed paper flaps are underneath. Using a rolling pin on the outside of the waxed paper, gently flatten the mixture evenly so that it thinly fills the envelope. Now, carefully turn the envelope over and unwrap the top of the meat but do not disturb it or remove it from the waxed paper. Using a sharp pizza cutter, score the meat in half the short way, then score each half into 3 strips. You will now have 6 scored strips on the waxed paper. Gently fold the paper flaps back over the meat, restoring the envelope. Repeat three times with the remaining meat. Place the 4 envelopes on a cookie sheet or any broad, flat container and place them in the freezer. To store, put the envelopes in a sealed plastic bag after the meat has frozen

To cook, simply unwrap and break off the desired number of frozen strips and, *without thawing*, fry them in a pan coated with:

lecithin pan coating (page 214)

until crisp as bacon on both sides. To prevent the strips from breaking, make sure the first side is crisp before turning. Drain thoroughly on paper towels. *Makes 2 dozen "bacon" strips.*

NOTE: Like bacon, these strips contain a high proportion of salt. So, for your health's sake, they should be eaten only in small quantities.

VARIATION Use ground beef instead of pork. Omit the sugar. Instead, add:

½ *teaspoon ground black pepper*

Fry as for pork strips.

Chapter 10

Soups That Don't Come
in a Can or Box

"Is it soup yet?" has to be one of the more aggravating cries heard on TV commercials. The message is obvious. Mom, who is not smart enough to make soup on her own, is conned into thinking she is doing it by mixing a dry, processed powder with water and briefly boiling the resultant liquid. This type of product or those made by stirring boiling water into a powder in a teacup cannot begin to approach the good flavor and nutrition of the delicious start-from-scratch variety. Nor can condensed canned soups, which are often highly salted and filled with soggy, overcooked vegetables and noodles. Besides tasting better, homemade soups also cost less and contain no harmful preservatives or artificial flavors or coloring.

Homemade soup falls into two categories: *Leftovers soups,* which give you the chance to clean out the refrigerator, feed the family inexpensively, and get a nutritious meal all at the same time. Talk about convenience foods! And *classic soups,* in which a recipe is followed to produce an identical, predictable result each time. Obviously, the leftovers soups are more fun. But whether you are making that kind or one of the classic soups, the following tips will help:

· Cook the ingredients as quickly as possible. Yes, grandma simmered them for hours—and destroyed many of the nutrients.

If possible, use a pressure cooker. You'll get all the flavor of long-simmered soups and the vitamins of quick cooking.

· Add ingredients in their proper order. Thus, tough meat should be cooked longer than tender fresh vegetables. So start with the meat and add the vegetables at the proper interval during the cooking.

· With cream soups, make a concentrate that is thoroughly cooked, then add the thickening and milk just before serving. This will avoid burned pots and soup that tastes like old cigars.

· Be imaginative with herbs. Especially with soups made from leftovers! After you get the knack of making a good basic cream soup, try, for example, cream of cabbage with dillweed or cream of watercress with basil—or would you believe cream of leftover hash-brown potatoes with onions, garlic, and thyme?

With a pressure cooker, you can make delicious and nutritious homemade soup for lunch or dinner in little more time than it takes to open a can, add water, and heat the contents. Without a pressure cooker, it takes only a little longer.

Recipes in this chapter include:

Favorite Vegetable-Beef Soup

In a pressure cooker, if possible, or in a large pot, brown:

½ pound beef, cut into ¾-inch cubes, OR ½ pound small compressed cubes or balls of ground beef

When done, add:

2 *cubed carrots*	1 *tablespoon tamari sauce*
2 *cubed onions*	2 *dashes of Tabasco sauce*
2 *cubed medium potatoes*	1 *teaspoon paprika*
1 *8-ounce can stewed*	½ *teaspoon garlic powder*
tomatoes OR, *better yet,*	¼ *teaspoon marjoram*
2 *diced fresh tomatoes*	1½ *quarts water*

Cook in the pressure cooker for 10 minutes, or bring to a boil in the soup pot and simmer for about 30 minutes. Then add:

2 *tablespoons flour dissolved in ½ cup water*

Add this slowly, stirring constantly to thicken. Yum!

Good soup of this kind always has a small amount of oil on top for richness. So if you've used extra-lean beef in making your soup, stir in just before serving:

1 *tablespoon vegetable oil*

If the meat tended to be somewhat fatty, however, you may wish to skim off some of the fat before serving. Too much makes the soup greasy. *Makes approximately 3 quarts.*

VARIATIONS   Skip the meat and add other vegetables instead, such as string beans, shredded greens, and so on. If you like a thin soup, omit the flour-and-water thickening.

Chicken Gumbo

Start with chicken and stock. The best way to get this is to cook in a pressure cooker for about 15 minutes:

a leftover well-picked	1 *quart water*
chicken carcass	

You'll be amazed at how much meat still remains to be picked from the bones. If you can't do this, buy some inexpensive chicken parts and cook them. Or, if necessary, use leftover chicken and bouillon. In any case . . .

Combine:

1 *quart chicken stock*
1 *cup diced or shredded cooked chicken*
½ *cup drained canned or frozen corn* OR *cooked rice*
1 *chopped onion*
½ *stalk celery, diced*
2 *diced fresh tomatoes*

½ *cup fresh or frozen okra, sliced*
salt to taste
½ *teaspoon thyme (this is vital!)*
a dash of Tabasco OR *1 or 2 shakes of pepper for zest*

The secret of gumbo is okra, which thickens and flavors the soup, and thyme, which gives it its distinctive gumbo taste. Cook in a pressure cooker for 5 minutes, or bring to a boil and simmer for about 15 minutes. Add:

1 *tablespoon vegetable oil*

if needed for richness. *Makes about 2 quarts.*

VARIATIONS Try substituting 1 small can shrimp for the chicken, using chicken stock. Or use beef stock and cubed beef instead of the chicken and chicken stock.

Clam Chowder

Chowder is a thick soup, often with a cream base, often containing seafood. Here is the way to make one of the five thousand genuine, original versions of New England clam chowder.

In a pressure cooker or in a large pot, combine:

1 *cup chicken stock (see opposite page)*
1 *diced carrot*
2 *diced medium potatoes*
2 *diced onions*

1 *7-ounce can clams or minced clams*
1 *teaspoon tamari sauce*
salt and pepper to taste
¼ *teaspoon thyme*

Cook all of the ingredients in the pressure cooker for 5 minutes, or simmer until done. Slowly add:

¼ *cup flour dissolved in ½ cup water*

stirring constantly and cooking until thickened. When thickened, slowly add:

1 *quart milk*

Heat through before serving. For extra creaminess, dissolve:

¼ *cup instant nonfat dry milk*

in the whole milk before adding it to the soup. Serve this and all chowders topped with a pat of butter. *Makes about 2 quarts.*

VARIATION   Substitute shredded fish for the clams. This is a good way to use leftover fish. Canned tuna, however, doesn't work very well.

Corn Chowder

Here's another New England-style chowder recipe for people who don't like clams.

In a pressure cooker or in a large pot, combine:

1 *cup chicken stock* (see page 80)	*kernels cut from 2 ears fresh corn*
1 *diced carrot*	1 *teaspoon tamari sauce*
2 *diced medium potatoes*	*salt and pepper to taste*
2 *diced onions*	½ *teaspoon paprika*
1 *8-ounce can corn* OR 1 *10-ounce package frozen corn* OR	⅛ *teaspoon sage*

Cook all of the ingredients in the pressure cooker for 5 minutes, or simmer until done. Mix until dissolved:

¼ *cup flour*	½ *cup water*

Slowly add the flour-water mixture to the soup, stirring constantly and cooking until thickened. When thickened, slowly add:

1 *quart milk*

Heat through before serving. For extra creaminess, dissolve:

¼ *cup instant nonfat dry milk*

in the whole milk before adding it to the soup. Serve topped with a pat of butter. *Makes about 2 quarts.*

Gazpacho

Here's the ideal gourmet soup to serve when it's too hot to cook.

Coarsely dice and place in a blender:

2 *fresh tomatoes*	*bits of fresh basil, garlic,*
½ *green pepper*	*parsley to taste*
½ *carrot*	2 *tablespoons vegetable*
½ *onion*	*oil*
½ *cucumber, peeled if skin is*	2 *tablespoons apple cider*
thick or waxed	*vinegar*
salt and pepper to taste	1½ *cups cold chicken broth*

Whip until thoroughly pureed, pour into bowls, top with croutons, and serve. *Makes approximately 1 quart.*

VARIATION Substitute cold plain yogurt for the cold chicken broth, omitting the oil, vinegar, and croutons.

Chapter 11

Dinner Meats That Leave

Your Budget Intact

THERE ARE TWO problems involved with buying meat. This important food is becoming more and more popular as a main dish, not just in this country, but everywhere. So prices are going up because of increasing demand. Prices are also rising because of the increasing cost of raising and processing the animals.

The second problem in buying meat is the fact that much of it contains undesirable chemicals and additives. For example:

- Ham—Water Added. That's the way ham is labeled in the market. But how many people realize that ham has been puffed up with water up to 10 percent of its weight? A harmful additive? No. But who wants to pay ham prices for water?

- Hamburger can contain up to 30 percent fat. This means high prices for waste that will just cook off. Some butchers stain the fat with blood to make it appear lean. Some add a bit of water to beef up (forgive the expression) the weight.

- You've heard of DES. Diethylstilbestrol. It is a synthetic female hormone fed to steers. It makes them retain water and gain weight fast. The meat packers love it because they can "finish" an animal faster and for greater profit. But you are getting watery meat. Worse, DES is a proven carcinogen. And it has been banned in some countries because of claims that it emasculates men who eat beef raised on it. How do you like the fact that beef raised on DES is banned in over twenty countries—but not America?

- Bacon, ham, and other meat products are often treated or "cured" with sodium nitrate or sodium nitrite. In the presence of amines, chemical compounds that occur naturally in meat, nitrites react in the stomach to form nitrosamines, which cause mutagenic changes. They are highly suspected as carcinogens. Why use nitrates and nitrites? Once upon a time, they preserved food. Now, with refrigeration and freezing, many experts say they aren't needed. They are used to give ham, bacon, dried beef, and so on that nice reddish color. Useful, huh?

- Then consider chickens. They no longer run around the farmyard clucking. Instead, they are packed into cages and fed mechanically, never really moving around until they are killed. Over seven hundred additives are in use in various poultry and cattle feeds. These include antibiotics and growth stimulants, many of which may cause cancer and which can possibly be passed on in the meat to you, the consumer.

What can you do? For starters, you can write to the FDA and USDA and raise a bit of hell! But if past experience is a teacher, that won't do much good. One could get the impression that these agencies seem to favor big business over the consumer just a teeny bit. So hit 'em where it hurts. Here's how:

- Buy your beef from an inspected local grower. This means you will need a freezer for meat storage, but your savings will pay for it within a year or less. DON'T BUY FROM A LOCAL FREEZER PLAN—BUY FROM A LOCAL MEAT RAISER! Shop around; you can find them, even little more than an hour's drive from most big cities. And the prices for a side or a hindquarter of beef will amaze you. So will the convenience of "shopping" from your own freezer. Why buy from a local grower? Because you can find out what he feeds his animals and eliminate DES and other undesirable things.

- If possible, buy pork from the same meat raiser. Many of these small shops also raise pigs.

- Chickens can be purchased at the farm. Again, if you have a freezer you can get a six-months' supply all at once.

Won't this cost a lot? Surprisingly, not usually. Local slaughter-houses have to compete with the big markets and are frequently cheaper, especially if you buy in bulk. Compare the prices, pound for pound, with what you pay at the supermarket.

FISH

Fish is an excellent source of protein, though it is no longer a low-budget dish used in place of meat. However, the oils in fish, unlike the fat in most meats, do not tend to raise the blood choles-terol. The protein is easily digested and complete in essential amino acids. Of all the protein foods, fish is among the most likely to be relatively uncontaminated. However, fish do live in polluted waters. And some of the pollution can be passed on to you.

Here are a few tips on buying fish:

- Stick to saltwater fish whenever possible, because the chance of chemical pollution is less than for freshwater fish.
- Try to buy truly fresh fish. If you have a good local fish market that specializes in selling fresh fish that is delivered frequently, count yourself lucky!
- When you can't get fresh fish, buy frozen fish that is untreated with chemicals. You can tell by reading the label.

SOY-PROTEIN MEAT EXTENDERS

Soy protein can be used to stretch your meat budget in many ways. The protein in soybeans is *good* protein. It is complete in that it has all of the essential amino acids needed to sustain life. However, it is slightly weak in a few of these amino acids, so if you wish, you can improve the protein in soybeans by serving or mixing them with corn products, bran, or whole wheat.

Soybeans come in various forms: whole, chopped as grits, or in flours. The flour even comes in the form of full-fat or defatted.

From a nutritional standpoint, the whole fat has some advantages; but if you are on a diet or wish to cut your fat intake, you can use the defatted.

Unfortunately, soybeans don't have a taste that has universal appeal. So most people prefer to use them as a natural additive to other foods. Thus, by mixing them with beef in proportions in which the beef flavor dominates, the soybeans add much value and nutrition to the diet.

There is another problem with soybeans, and that is they take forever to cook. You can avoid this by buying the grits or the flour; or, if you want to save money, you can buy whole beans and grind them yourself.

Finally, when used as a meat extender, soybeans are more acceptable when strong flavors are used. Tamari sauce helps give them a beefy flavor. Tomato sauce makes them blend in with the meat. Hearty gravy completely disguises the taste.

When using soybeans as a meat extender, keep these tips in mind:

· Be sure the beans are thoroughly cooked, or they will be tough. Using the flour avoids this.

· Use seasonings in, as well as on, the meat wherever possible.

· Use the beans in a relatively small proportion to that of the meat. Twenty-five percent is about tops.

· Add water to the beans to make the dish the proper consistency. Keep in mind that the dry flour or grits will absorb water from the meat that must be replaced.

What dishes can be extended with soybeans and water? Chicken croquettes, fish patties, pork patties, meatballs, hamburger. And don't forget that extended hamburger can be used wherever regular hamburger is used, so that in dishes such as meat loaf, you can actually extend the meat twice—once with the soybeans and water and then again with bread crumbs and other standard meat loaf ingredients.

Here are the recipes that appear in this chapter:

Extended Hamburger

You've seen it in the supermarket under various names, but it all comes down to the same thing: ground beef plus soy protein plus water, at a somewhat reduced price. The theory is great, but why pay beef prices for soybeans and water? Make your own and save the difference!

In a blender, grind until it is the consistency of fine cornmeal:

enough soybeans to yield ½ cup soybean flour

In a large bowl, put:

½ cup soybean flour   *¾ cup water*

Mix thoroughly and let sit for 5 minutes. Then mix in:

1 pound ground beef

working it with a heavy spoon until you have a uniform mixture. This is ready to use in either hamburger patties or meat loaf. *Makes 1½ pounds.*

For an extra meaty flavor, add:

2 tablespoons tamari sauce

as you mix the meat and soybean flour, using 2 tablepoons less water.

HINT: For an even easier extended hamburger, use already ground soy flour, available at a health food store. Buying it loose costs less than buying it in a package.

Hamburger Steaks

One reason the price of steak is so high is that a steer only has a few pounds of it, but many pounds of tough muscle that must be ground up. Here's the way to turn hamburger into "steaks" and make the family rave.

Start with good-quality, lean ground beef.

In a bowl, mix:

1 *pound ground beef*   ½ *teaspoon garlic powder*
1 *tablespoon tamari sauce*

Divide into 3 or 4 equal servings. Place each on a square of waxed paper. Fold the paper up over the meat, then under on each side so that the meat is in an envelope the size of the patty you want to make. Using the heel of your hand, firmly shape the meat into a rectangle, filling the waxed-paper envelope and pushing out all of the air. Unwrap and broil until the desired doneness has been reached. No salt is needed. *Serves 3 or 4.*

Basic Hamburger 'n' Gravy

Here is the most versatile convenience food involving meat. You can make it in quantity when ground beef is cheap and freeze it in small amounts to be quickly thawed and used in one of many dishes. The whole idea is to get a hamburger–brown gravy combination without canned gravy, which contains dubious ingredients. The directions are very important. Here they are.

Coat a large frying pan with:

lecithin pan coating (page 214) OR *a little vegetable oil*

Bring it to medium heat. Add:

 1 *pound lean ground beef*

breaking it up with a fork. Grill over medium heat, stirring with a flat turner until all of the juice cooks away and the meat drippings begin to brown nicely. Spoon off any excess fat while browning. Then add:

¼ *cup chopped onion*   1 *tablespoon tamari sauce*
½ *teaspoon garlic powder*

Continue to cook, still stirring, still adding to the brown gravy base. After cooking for a total of about 20 minutes, and after the pan is thoroughly coated with rich brown drippings, stir in:

 1 *cup water*

constantly scraping the pan with the turner to dissolve all of the brown drippings that have adhered to the pan. (This is where the lecithin pan coating helps.)

When the mixture is boiling, add a little more water if necessary; you should have cooked hamburger bits with onions in a savory juice. Using a mixture of 2 parts water to 1 part flour, thicken the mixture to taste. That's all there is to it. *Makes a little over 2 cups.*

VARIATIONS   Add 1 tablespoon paprika for a richer gravy. Or add ½ cup chopped mushrooms.

What can you do with this mixture?

- You can serve it over toast points as is, along with a tossed salad for a quick supper.
- You can mix it with 2 cups cooked noodles or rice for a fast main dish.
- Put it in a casserole and add ½ cup each cooked sliced carrots, cooked peas, and cooked chopped green peppers. Cover with a thick layer of fluffy mashed potatoes. And bake until heated through and golden on top. Presto—instant shepherd's pie!
- Mix it with 2 cups tomato sauce for a hearty, meaty spaghetti sauce.

Barbecued Burger

Here's a delicious Pennsylvania Dutch dish that predates the now popular sloppy Joes and is served in the same way. It's easy to make in quantity and may be frozen in small amounts until needed.

In a large frying pan, heat:

1 tablespoon vegetable oil

Add and cook until brown:

1 pound ground beef

Add:

½ cup chopped onion　　　　*¼ cup chopped celery*
¼ cup chopped green pepper

Stir-fry until the vegetables are tender, then add:

1 8-ounce can tomato sauce　　*1½ teaspoons Worcester-*
¼ cup catsup　　　　　　　　*shire sauce*
1 tablespoon vinegar　　　　*1 teaspoon salt*
1 tablespoon sugar OR　　　　*¼ teaspoon pepper*
*　honey*

Mix well and simmer for 20 minutes. Serve on hamburger buns or over toast points or hot buttered noodles. *Serves 6.*

Tamari Chicken Barbecue

Here's an unusual dish that will win you praise yet is easy to fix even when unexpected company drops in—providing, of course, that you have some chicken on hand. Frozen cut-up chicken works fine. No need to defrost, but you do have to be able to separate the pieces, and you will have to cook it longer. This recipe is enough for:

2 large chicken breasts, split OR *the equivalent in other pieces*

In a fairly flat bowl, put:

¼ *cup vegetable oil*	4 *drops Tabasco sauce*
1 *teaspoon liquid lecithin*	¼ *teaspoon garlic powder*
2 *tablespoons tamari sauce*	

Whip with a fork. This will *not* work without the lecithin, which emulsifies the water-based tamari and the oil into a smooth mixture.

Dip each piece of chicken into the mix and coat well. Bake, breasts and thighs meat side up, in a shallow pan for 45 minutes in a pre-heated 350-degree oven, basting occasionally with any remaining sauce. Or cook over a charcoal grill, turning the chicken often enough to prevent burning. If you bake the chicken in the oven, just before serving crisp it for a moment under the broiler. *Serves 4.*

Dilute the drippings with water and save for soup stock, or use them for making gravy. Here's how to make the gravy.

Take the chicken out of the baking pan and put it in the warm oven on a serving platter. Shake together in a small jar:

¼ *cup water*	1 *tablespoon flour*

Into the baking pan, put:

¾ *cup water*	*salt to taste*

Stir over medium heat, scraping all of the brown drippings from the pan. After it starts to boil, slowly stir in the flour-water mixture. Stir constantly until thickened.

VARIATIONS Use with fish fillets instead of chicken. Or, for an Italian-style barbecued chicken, omit the tamari sauce and use instead: 3 tablespoons vinegar, 1 teaspoon salt, and a pinch of oregano.

Old-fashioned Scrapple

Here's an old dish that the thrifty Pennsylvania Dutch have made famous. It's a great convenience food to have on hand and inexpensive to make. The name comes from the fact that it was originally made from pork scraps, but you can easily make it from good pork sausage. Buy the kind that is additive-free. Be a label reader!

Here are the steps.

Cut into 4 sections:

a 1-pound roll pork sausage

Cook in a pressure cooker for 20 minutes (or cover and cook until well done) with:

2 cups water

Remove the pieces of meat and put aside. Pour the liquid into a bowl. Let the grease rise to the top and skim it off.

Grind the meat along with 1 cup of the reserved liquid in a blender.

Using the uncovered pot of your already used pressure cooker, bring to a boil the remaining liquid plus enough water to make 2 cups. Stirring constantly, add:

1 cup cornmeal

Reduce the heat and stir for about 5 minutes, or until very thick.

Then add the ground meat mixture plus:

1 teaspooon salt	*¼ teaspoon ground black pepper*

Mix together thoroughly.

Pour the mixture into a greased 8-by-4-by-2½-inch *aluminum foil* loaf pan, cool, then chill in the refrigerator overnight, uncovered to prevent condensation of water on the top of the loaf. For easy unmolding, pull the flexible sides and ends of the pan slightly away from the scrapple and turn the loaf out onto a plate. To serve, slice it in pieces ½ inch thick, and panfry the slices in a frying pan coated with:

> lecithin pan coating (page 214)

until golden brown on both sides. Do not turn until the first side is crisp or the slice of scrapple may fall apart. Wrap and store any unused portion in the refrigerator. *Makes 2 pounds, or about 16 slices.*

VARIATIONS   Substitute 1 pound ground beef for the pork, adding 1 tablespoon tamari sauce and omitting the salt.

HINT: The folks who grow up eating pork scrapple often serve it with catsup or with applesauce or even topped with honey or maple syrup. It was originally a breakfast food; but with rising meat prices, it makes excellent extended meat for dinner.

Meat Loaf Mix

Here's a handy meat loaf mix you can make ahead of time, then use as needed.

In a warm oven, dry:

> stale bread slices

Grind them into bread crumbs in your blender or food processor. To each cup of bread crumbs, in a bowl, add:

½ cup instant nonfat dry milk	1 tablespoon dried onion
1 teaspoon garlic powder	flakes
1 teaspoon salt	1 tablespoon dried sweet
1 teaspoon paprika	pepper flakes
1 teaspoon basil	

Mix thoroughly and store in a jar or plastic bag. There is no need to refrigerate this because all of the ingredients are dried.

To make a quick meat loaf, simply put in a large bowl:

1 pound ground beef

Add:

1 egg   *1 cup Meat Loaf Mix*
½ cup water

Blend thoroughly with a fork, adding more water if necessary to get a workable mixture. Bake in a preheated 350-degree oven until done through, or about 45 minutes. *Serves 6.*

HINT: The secret of good meat loaf is to pack it tight enough so that no air bubbles give it a loose texture. To do this, line a loaf pan with an oversized piece of plastic wrap. Spoon the meat loaf mixture onto the plastic, using the loaf pan as a mold. Every increasing inch or so, use the back of a heavy spoon to press out air pockets. When all of the mixture is packed in, place a shallow baking pan upside down on top of the loaf pan, flip over the whole business carefully, lift off the loaf pan, peel off the plastic, and your meat loaf is ready to bake.

VARIATIONS   If you like to serve your meat loaf with tomato sauce, add ½ teaspoon oregano to each cup of bread crumbs in addition to the other seasonings. If you like a mushroom topping, add ½ teaspoon marjoram in addition to the other seasonings. For a beefier flavor, add 1 tablespoon tamari sauce when you add the water and egg and omit the salt from the Meat Loaf Mix.

Inexpensive Convenience Coatings

Ask yourself why Shake 'n Bake coating mixes are so popular. The answer is simple. They add a delightful flavor and extend the meat by keeping in moisture. You can make your own. Here are several variations. Store them like bread crumbs.

Basic Coating

In a blender or food processor, put:

1 *cup dry bread crumbs*	½ *teaspoon basil*
½ *teaspoon salt*	½ *teaspoon dried celery*
¼ *teaspoon ground black*	*leaves*
pepper	½ *teaspoon paprika*
½ *teaspoon garlic powder*	

Blend until fine. To use, simply place in a plastic bag, add the meat, close the top without letting out too much of the air, shake until the meat is coated, place the meat in a pan, and bake until done.

Health Food Coating

In a bowl, mix:

1 *cup raw wheat germ*	1 *teaspoon paprika*
½ *teaspoon garlic powder*	½ *teaspoon salt*

Use in the same manner as the basic mix.

Coating for Beef or Veal

To make a good coating for small beef or veal cutlets, use:

> *either of the above mixes*

but add:

½ *teaspoon marjoram* OR *oregano*

Bake in a preheated 300-degree oven for 1 hour. *Coating is sufficient for 6 to 8 cutlets.*

Coating for Chicken

Use:

> *either of the above mixes*

but add:

½ *teaspoon thyme*   ½ *teaspoon sage*

Bake in a preheated 350-degree oven for about 50 minutes, or until done. *Coating is sufficient for 1 frying chicken, cut into pieces.*

Coating for Pork Chops

Use:

> *either of the above mixes*

but add:

½ *teaspoon dried tarragon* OR ¼ *teaspoon allspice*

Bake in a preheated 350-degree oven until done through, about 45 minutes. *Coating is sufficient for 6 thick chops.*

Fantastic Fish

Fish is a tender and delicate food that should be cooked accordingly. Heavy coatings and deep frying mask the excellent flavor of fresh fish. Here's an easy way to cook those convenient fillets your fish market man will cut for you.

Coat a cookie sheet or shallow baking pan with:

> *lecithin pan coating* (page 214)

Arrange:

> *fillets of any fresh saltwater fish, such as bluefish, perch, sole, scrod, pollack, or halibut*

Brush the fish lightly with:

> *vegetable oil*

Season lightly with:

> *salt and pepper*

Garnish with:

a bit of basil   *a generous dash of paprika*
garlic powder to taste

Broil 5 or 6 inches from heat until done through and golden. Allow 8 to 10 minutes for thin fillets and up to 15 minutes for fillets that are 1 inch thick.

Serve with lemon wedges and wait for the raves!

Chapter 12

Vegetables and Fruits with More

Vitamins, Fewer Pesticides

"WITH DIPHENYL, PEEL UNSUITABLE FOR CONSUMPTION." These words of warning must be stamped on citrus fruit grown in the U.S. and exported to some European countries, including Germany and Italy. It's frightening to realize that the big food corporations have succeeded in getting dangerous chemicals "approved" for American consumption while they are banned elsewhere. Germany has banned the use of mineral oil as a coating for produce since 1938. In America, it is permitted on raw fruits and vegetables. Oranges, shipped green, are dyed with various coloring agents, which are, one after the other, declared "safe," then later banned, as was the case with red 32, which was replaced with red 2, which has since also been replaced. Dyed American oranges are banned by Canada, Great Britain, and other countries.

Old potatoes may be dyed to make them appear to be "new" potatoes. Until recently, sweet potatoes were dyed into yams— again, banned for import into Canada but allowed in the U.S. until 1968.

Chemicals in our vegetables and fruits basically break down into these types: artificial coloring agents; flavor enhancers, especially MSG, often found in canned vegetables; excess salt, again found in canned vegetables; sugar, which is put unnecessarily into so many things, even vegetables; preservatives, which keep the vegetable or fruit from getting moldy or sprouting and otherwise extend its

99

shelf life; and pesticide residues. These latter are of two types: (a) systemic; and (b) those that coat the outside of the vegetable. Systemic insecticides give lettuce the chance to bite back by making the whole plant poisonous to the bugs. Care to eat it yourself? Sorry—you can't tell whether a plant has been treated, and you can't wash it off. Insecticides on the outside of the plant can, to some extent, be removed.

Here's the way to avoid most of these chemicals:

· Buy fresh fruits and vegetables whenever possible. And within that framework, buy those locally grown and from the smallest farm possible. Produce from such suppliers doesn't have to be able to survive long-distance shipping or weary days on market shelves. So it isn't sprayed as much. Unless you know that the vegetables are organically grown, wash them thoroughly in a solution of ¼ cup vinegar to 1 gallon water. This helps to loosen persistent oily sprays used as the base for insecticides and also helps to remove the oils and waxes that are used to make the fruits and vegetables "prettier."

· As second choice, use frozen vegetables. They are likely to have fewer chemical additives and residues than canned, although in 1970–71, the Agricultural Marketing Service discovered about 39 million pounds of fruits and vegetables in both freezing and canning plants that were below U.S. standards because the products contained "excessive foreign materials—such as worms, insects, oil, mud, rot, rust or paint flakes—or because the products had been packed under unsanitary conditions."

· Best of all, grow your own. Even city dwellers can make a small backyard plot produce a respectable salad garden. And it's fun and easy to grow delicious sprouts in your kitchen.

Here are the recipes that are included in this chapter:

A Festive Fruit Dip Bowl

Here's a recipe that you can vary to suit your taste and the seasons. The basic thing is the dip:

1 pound cottage cheese   *¼ cup honey*
1 teaspoon pure vanilla extract

Whip all ingredients in a blender or food processor, scraping down the sides of the container frequently. Keep whipping until you get a creamy, smooth mixture.

Place the dip in an attractive bowl, cover, and chill for several hours. *Makes 2¼ cups.*

Serve on a large platter surrounded by fresh fruit in season. Be sure to try peeled orange slices, peeled tangerine sections, apple and pear slices (dipped in lemon juice to retard discoloration), large strawberries, melon slices. The list could go on and on. And why not?

Party Vegetable Dip

Here's a dip for vegetables that needs only a bottle of good homemade wine to make a party.

Whip in a blender or food processor, scraping down the sides of the container frequently:

1 pound cottage cheese   *1 teaspoon basil*
½ cup plain yogurt   *½ teaspoon dillweed*
1 teaspoon garlic powder

Keep whipping until you get a creamy, smooth mixture. Chill, covered, for several hours to allow permeation of the herb flavors and serve with assorted raw vegetables such as celery and carrot sticks, radishes, cauliflowerets, cucumber slices, and red and green pepper strips. *Makes 2½ cups.*

String Beans Almondine

You've eaten them at fancy restaurants, but the nuts were probably soggy. Here's how to make your own and come on as a gourmet make-it-yourself cook.

In a small frying pan, heat:

1 *tablespoon vegetable oil*

Quickly brown:

¼ cup raw slivered almonds

stirring constantly. Drain on paper towels and set aside.

Cook:

1 *pound fresh sliced string beans*

until done through but slightly crunchy. The best way to do this is to use a pressure cooker, just allowing the pressure to rise, then bringing it down under cold water at once.

Into the drained, hot beans, stir:

1 *tablespoon Extended Butter*   *salt to taste*
  (page 211)

and, just before serving, stir in the reserved almonds. *Serves 6.*

VARIATION   Many people consider it a real improvement to substitute ¼ cup raw pumpkin seeds for the almonds. These pop as they cook in the oil, so be careful. But the taste is marvelous.

Squash in Tomato Sauce

If you have a garden, chances are you have too much squash. Here's a good way to make an excess supply of yellow summer squash disappear fast.

Coarsely dice into 1-inch cubes:

2 *small or 1 medium yellow squash*

In a frying pan, heat:

2 *tablespoons vegetable oil*

Add the squash and:

1 *finely chopped garlic clove*   ½ *teaspoon salt (or to taste)*
(or to taste)

Stir fry for 10 minutes, or until the squash is just done through. Add:

1 *small can tomato sauce*

Stir, heat through, and serve. *Makes 3 servings.*

Zucchini Casserole

This recipe was invented when company dropped in for dinner and all that was available was a zucchini squash, some natural cheese, fresh mushrooms—and luck.

Onto a large piece of waxed paper, slice paper thin:

1 *medium zucchini*

Onto the same paper, but in a separate pile, slice paper thin:

¼ *pound fresh mushrooms*

Still onto the same paper, thinly slice:

6 *ounces medium to sharp Cheddar* OR *Colby cheese*

Oil a casserole, pouring into the bottom an extra:

1 *tablespoon vegetable oil*

Then make a thin layer of zucchini, topped with a thin layer of mushrooms, topped with a thin layer of cheese, dusted with:

a little salt   *a little basil*
a little garlic powder

Repeat the process—zucchini, mushrooms, cheese, seasonings—over and over, ending with the cheese and seasonings plus:

a sprinkle of paprika

Bake, uncovered, in a preheated 350-degree oven until a fork tells you the zucchini is done—about 20 minutes or so. Now, here is the secret. The resulting casserole will be much too runny to serve. To make it moist but not runny, turn off the oven and allow the casserole to stay in the closed warm oven until the liquid is reabsorbed—about another 15 minutes. *Serves 4 as a main dish.*

Serve with a large tossed salad and be amazed at how much people like zucchini!

VARIATION   Substitute 2 medium-sized onions sliced paper thin for the mushrooms.

Summer Jumble

Here is a recipe that you can enjoy only in summer when gardens abound.

In a frying pan or wok, heat:

 2 tablespoons vegetable oil

To this, add:

 1 cup small cauliflowerets

Stir fry for 2 minutes. Then add:

 1 large coarsely diced onion

Stir fry for 2 minutes. Then add:

 1 small coarsely diced summer   ½ finely chopped garlic clove
 squash

Continue to stir fry until just done, about an additional 3 minutes. Then add:

 2 large fresh diced tomatoes

Cover and steam 3 to 4 minutes. Add:

salt and pepper to taste

Serve and listen to the raves! *Makes 4 servings.*

VARIATIONS Infinite variations are possible. Add herbs to taste: Basil is nice; so is oregano; tarragon makes it French. And you can switch vegetables: Broccoli can fill in for the cauliflower, zucchini for the yellow squash, and so on. With summer vegetables, you can be as creative as you like!

Baked Broccoli and Mushrooms

This is another dish you may have had in a fine restaurant. The principle is simple. You make a mixture of compatible vegetables, butter, seasonings, and bread crumbs and bake it until it is brown and crunchy. Here's a good basic recipe.

In a frying pan, heat:

1 tablespoon vegetable oil

Stir fry just until done:

1 10-ounce package frozen broccoli, thawed and drained, OR *the equivalent*   *in coarsely chopped fresh broccoli*

Then add:

1 cup coarsely chopped mushrooms   *½ teaspoon garlic powder salt to taste*

Stir in:

crumbs from 2 slices blender- or food processor-chopped bread   *2 tablespoons Extended Butter* (page 211)

Bake, uncovered, in a small oiled baking dish in a preheated 350-degree oven until brown on top, for about 10 minutes. *Makes 4 servings.*

VARIATIONS   Variations are limited only by your imagination.

- Add 2 tablespoons grated Parmesan cheese and 1 teaspoon basil when you stir in the bread crumbs.
- Add 1 coarsely chopped onion, cooking it with the broccoli from the beginning.
- Substitute string beans for the broccoli.
- Substitute cauliflower for the broccoli.
- Substitute fresh zucchini for the broccoli.
- Add ¼ cup toasted sunflower seeds when you stir in the bread crumbs. (See directions for toasting slivered almonds on page 102.)
- Top with slices of sharp cheese.
- Substitute 1 cup leftover cooked rice for the bread crumbs.

You'll find that even the finicky vegetable eaters in your family will be eager to eat these delicious gourmet variations.

A Salad from Your Kitchen Garden

Livestock eat alfalfa and thrive on it. Scientists have isolated important growth factors in alfalfa. The protein in alfalfa is of high quality, and it is full of natural vitamins. Why don't more people eat it? As one woman said, "Alfalfa is for cows!" Fine. So call it by its classy English name—lucerne—and eat sprouted alfalfa seeds. They're delicious and they're fun and easy to grow right in your own kitchen. Here's the way to sprout alfalfa—pardon, lucerne—if you don't own or want to buy a seed sprouter.

Buy untreated alfalfa seeds at your health food store. They will cost about three to four dollars per pound. This may sound expensive, but you'll get a whole winter's greens for an average-sized family from just one pound.

In a glass of wrist-warm water, soak overnight:

2 tablespoons of alfalfa seeds

Discard the water by pouring the seeds into a very fine strainer. Spread the wet seeds on a moist white paper towel laid out on a cookie sheet. Cover with foil. Let sit for 2 days.

Now your seeds will be sprouted, just a bit. Put the sprouted seeds, without the paper towel, in a flat glass baking dish. Rinse and drain carefully. Spread the seeds on the bottom of the dish and cover the top with clear plastic wrap. Within 2 days, they will be about 1 inch long and intertwined enough to make them a fairly stable mass. This will then allow you to rinse and drain them without disturbing their growing pattern. Rinse and drain again at this point. Repeat after 4 days, then put the sprouts, uncovered, in a sunny window for 1 more day. This will make them grow to about an inch and a half long and develop tiny green, tasty leaves, which you will not get in jar-sprouted seeds.

At this point, rinse your sprouts thoroughly, washing away as many as possible of the tiny seed pods. These have no taste and are totally harmless, but most people prefer to discard them. Shake the sprouts dry and store them in a covered jar or plastic bag in the refrigerator. *Makes about 1 quart.*

To make your salad, treat the sprouts as you would fresh greens.

Dress with:

oil and vinegar to taste or *Cole Slaw and Potato Salad Dressing* (page 137)

An especially delicious salad can be made by adding to your sprouts, in any proportion to suit your taste:

chopped celery	*chopped tomatoes*
chopped onions	*chopped hard-cooked egg*

Along with the oil and vinegar you might add:

salt and pepper to taste	*a pinch of sugar*

Toss and serve.

VARIATIONS Instead of alfalfa, try sprouting mung beans. The sprouts are delicious when mixed with chopped onions and fresh vegetables and stir fried in the Chinese manner. An English favorite is a mixture of sprouted garden cress and mustard seeds, which are eaten on bread and butter. **BUT** . . . be sure to get untreated seeds at a health food store! Seeds from a garden shop may have been treated with chemicals to prevent fungus and would be harmful to eat.

Chapter 13

Starches from Scratch

FOR most families, a starch rounds out a meal. Common starches are corn, potatoes, rice, noodles, or breads. They're all easy to prepare at home but are expensive to buy in prepackaged mixes at the market. Just for fun, price a pound box of plain brown rice at your supermarket. Then price an equivalent amount of seasoned rice mix. If that doesn't make you a believer in making your own foods, nothing else will.

Corn

Whenever possible, buy fresh corn. Best of all, buy corn that has not been sprayed with chlorinated hydrocarbon pesticides. Don't squawk if you find an occasional worm in an ear. That may be a sign that the corn isn't loaded with bug spray. Rule: If it's not good enough for the bugs to eat, it's not good enough for you. Frozen corn is second best. Last is canned corn, but that's not bad if you buy it with no additives and use the liquid in your cooking to get all of the vitamins. Read the label.

Potatoes

If possible, get potatoes from a farmer who doesn't dust them to keep them from sprouting or dye them to make them pretty. Buy dirty potatoes. Prewashed ones cost a premium and have fewer vitamins. Avoid canned potatoes. They are often mushy, slippery, and too salty. You pay a big premium for frozen potato products. Ditto potato flakes. Buy fresh.

Rice

Natural brown rice does not have as long a shelf life as refined white rice. So manufacturers mill it, cook it, dry it, preserve it, and otherwise deplete the nutritive value. Buy brown rice and learn to cook it. It's easy, despite what you've heard. And if you've never much liked rice before, you're in for a surprise. Brown rice really tastes good!

Noodles

You can buy noodles with or without artificial coloring. It's pretty obvious what kind you should get. Read your label. Best of all, make your own. It's not all that hard, and it will build your ego as a do-it-yourself cook. Besides, you can even sneak in some safe "additives" that actually enhance the nutritive value.

Bread Dishes

Would you rather have mashed potatoes or Stove-Top Stuffing? Depends on your mood, of course. Either way, you can make your own. Unless you enjoy paying a lot of money for flavored bread cubes.

Here are the recipes contained in this chapter:

Nonfried French Fries

Everyone loves french-fried potatoes, but no one likes the cleanup. And not many people prefer the frozen variety over good homemade fries. But you can make your own inexpensively, with little cleanup, and as quickly as the rest of your meal.

For each person, scrub:

1 large potato

Don't bother to peel. Cut the potatoes into french-fry-size strips, remembering that cooking will cause some shrinkage; so don't slice them *too* thin, unless you want shoestring potatoes.

In a bowl, pour:

about 1 tablespoon vegetable oil for each potato

Add the potato strips, and, using a spoon, toss them, coating them lightly but thoroughly with the oil.

Spread the potato strips on a cookie sheet or sheets, not touching, and bake in a preheated 425-degree oven for about 10 minutes, or until brown. Turn the heat down to 350 degrees and bake, turning with a spatula occasionally, for another 20 to 30 minutes, or until done through. Salt and serve.

VARIATIONS   For a barbecued flavor, dust with a little paprika, a pinch of cayenne, and a little garlic and onion powder as well as the salt. For a health-food variety, coat with raw wheat germ before baking.

Perfect Brown Rice

Instant rice is uninspiring. It is almost as tasteless as store-bought white bread. And it is so easy to fix perfect brown rice! Here's how.

In a pressure cooker, heat:

1 tablespoon vegetable oil

Add:

1 cup brown rice

Stir. Let the rice brown slightly. Add:

2¼ cups water

Cook under manufacturer's recommended pressure for 20 minutes. Let the pressure drop by itself. Uncover the pot; stir the rice to allow the excess moisture to steam off. You will have fluffy, delicious rice. *Serves 4.*

NOTE: If you use short-grain rice, you may need 1 or 2 tablespoons less water.

Seasoned Rice Mixes

Seasoned Rice for Chicken

Mix together:

1 *cup brown rice*	1 *pinch of saffron*
½ *teaspoon garlic powder*	½ *teaspoon salt*
½ *teaspoon thyme*	⅛ *teaspoon ground black*
½ *teaspoon sage*	*pepper*
½ *teaspoon dried celery leaves*	

Cook according to the directions for Perfect Brown Rice (page 111). *Serves 4.*

Seasoned Rice for Beef

Mix together:

1 *cup brown rice*	½ *teaspoon salt*
½ *teaspoon marjoram*	⅛ *teaspoon ground black*
¼ *teaspoon garlic powder*	*pepper*
1½ *teaspoons dried onion flakes*	

Cook according to the directions for Perfect Brown Rice (page 111). *Serves 4.*

If you wish extra flavor, reduce the salt to ¼ teaspoon and, just before cooking, add:

1 *teaspoon tamari sauce*

Seasoned Rice for Pork

Mix together:

1 cup brown rice

½ teaspoon dillweed OR thyme

½ teaspoon paprika

¼ teaspoon dry mustard

½ teaspoon salt

⅛ teaspoon ground black pepper

Cook according to the directions for Perfect Brown Rice (page 111). *Serves 4.*

NOTE: For convenience, make several batches of the uncooked mixes in advance, storing them in small jars or small, sealed plastic bags. Then, when you want to serve rice, simply use the contents of one of your own homemade "packages." If you wish to prepare Seasoned Rice for Beef with tamari sauce, make up these advance mixes using the lower amount of salt.

Fried Rice

Cook:

any of the seasoned rice mixes (see opposite page)

If possible, allow the rice to cool thoroughly. Even better, chill it in the refrigerator for a few hours.

In a wok or heavy frying pan, heat:

2 tablespoons vegetable oil

Add:

½ cup chopped celery

½ cup chopped onion

½ cup chopped mushrooms

Using high heat, quickly stir fry the vegetables for about 3 minutes, or until just tender, then add the cold rice and continue to stir fry for about 5 minutes, or until the rice is heated through and slightly brown. *Serves 4.*

Homemade Noodles

These are a special treat to be used only when you want the very best—like today, for instance.

Place in a bowl and mix together thoroughly:

2 cups unbleached white flour   1 teaspoon salt
OR whole wheat flour OR half
and half

Make a well in the mixture and add:

2 eggs

Using a fork, work the eggs into the flour. Continue to work them in thoroughly until you get a firm dough. If necessary, add:

a little water

a drop or so at a time, continuing to work the dough.

Let the dough rest for a few minutes. Then, using a floured board, knead it until you get a satiny smooth dough that is downright sensuous to the touch.

Again, using a well-floured board and a rolling pin, roll out the dough. For lasagna noodles, make it fairly thick, about 1/16 inch. For fettucini, make it a bit thinner. For linguine, very thin. Experiment.

There are two ways to cut the dough. One is to let it dry for 20 minutes, dust it with flour, roll it up like a jelly roll, and slice through it. This is best for spaghetti or other thin noodles. For broad noodles, simply cut with a pizza cutter right on the floured board. *Yields about 1 pound noodles.*

To cook, bring to a boil:

4 quarts water

Before putting in the noodles, add to the cooking water:

1 tablespoon vegetable oil

to help keep the noodles from sticking to the bottom of the pan and each other. Boil, uncovered, stirring occasionally, for about 10 minutes or until done to taste. Drain in a colander and serve with your favorite sauce. *Makes 4 or 5 servings.*

Food Processor Technique

Your food processor makes homemade noodles a snap to make because it does both the mixing and kneading in one step, in just a few minutes.

Using the steel blade, put in the processor container:

2 *cups unbleached white*	1 *teaspoon salt*
flour OR *whole wheat flour*	2 *eggs*
OR *half and half*	

Process for a few seconds. If the mixture is crumbly, and it will be unless you use huge eggs, while the processor is running, through the chute slowly add:

cold water, a teaspoonful at a time

Process until the mixture forms a firm ball. Then remove from the container to a floured board, allow the dough to rest for a few minutes, then roll out and cut according to the directions above.

VARIATIONS   Add seasonings right to the flour and salt for extra flavor. One-quarter teaspoon garlic or onion powder, basil or oregano, or even a pinch of cayenne. To sneak in a little nutrition, add a tablespoon or so of brewer's yeast powder or, if you use unbleached white flour, a tablespoon of raw wheat germ. Making noodles is an art, so be creative!

Ground-Beef Assister

You can't make Hamburger Helper because you can't get the necessary chemical additives. But, then, you don't need them either. You're not going to make a product that requires a long shelf life. Neither do you need to spend money on advertising, fancy packaging, or profits for stockholders, commissions for salespeople, or markups for merchants. So save money. Make homemade Ground Beef Assister instead. Combined with a pound of ground beef, each recipe makes a tasty skillet supper your family will love.

TIP: Tear off as many sheets of waxed paper, each about 1½ feet long, as the number you wish to fix of make-ahead packages of these recipes. Arrange them on a table. Go from sheet to sheet, piling one set of ingredients on each in turn. Then dump each sheet into a separate plastic bag, seal with a twist tie, and voilà! You're in the food-manufacturing business!

Italian-Style Assister

On each sheet of paper, mix together:

8 *ounces uncooked broad noodles*	¼ *teaspoon oregano*
	½ *teaspoon garlic powder*
1 *tablespoon dried onion flakes*	½ *teaspoon basil*
	½ *teaspoon salt*

To cook, lightly brown in a large frying pan:

1 *pound ground beef*

Add:

3½ *cups water*

and bring to a boil. Then add:

1 *package of mix*	1 *8-ounce can tomato sauce*

Let simmer, stirring often, for about 20 minutes, or until the noodles are done to taste. Sprinkle with grated Parmesan cheese if desired. *Serves 4 as a main dish.*

Stroganoff-Style Assister

On each sheet of paper, mix together:

8 *ounces uncooked medium*   ½ *teaspoon paprika*
  noodles   1 *teaspoon salt*
1 *cup instant nonfat dry milk*   ⅛ *teaspoon ground black*
1 *tablespoon dried onion flakes*   *pepper*

To cook, lightly brown in a large frying pan:

1 *pound ground beef*   1 *small can mushrooms*
1 *cup sliced mushrooms* OR   *with liquid*

Then add:

4 *cups water*   1 *tablespoon vinegar*

Bring it to a boil, then add:

1 *package of mix*

Let simmer, stirring often, for about 20 minutes, or until the noodles are done to taste. *Serves 4 as a main dish.*

Macaroni and Cheese Assister

On each sheet of paper, mix together:

8 *ounces uncooked elbow*   1 *teaspoon paprika*
  or small shell macaroni   1 *teaspoon salt*
1 *cup instant nonfat dry milk*   ⅛ *teaspoon ground black*
¼ *teaspoon thyme*   *pepper*
½ *teaspoon dry mustard*

To cook, lightly brown in a large frying pan:

1 *pound ground beef*

Add:

4 *cups water*

Bring to a boil, then add:

> 1 *package of mix*

Let simmer, stirring often, for about 20 minutes, or until the noodles are done to taste. Then add:

> 1 *cup grated sharp Cheddar cheese*

Let simmer gently, stirring frequently, until the cheese is evenly melted through. *Serves 4 as a main dish.*

For further ideas, see "Variations on All Assisters Using Pasta" (page 120).

Rice and Beef

Cook:

> 1 *cup Seasoned Rice Mix for Beef* (page 112)

In a frying pan, lightly brown:

> 1 *pound ground beef*

Add the cooked seasoned rice for beef plus:

> 1 *tablespoon tamari sauce*

Stir and serve. *Serves 4 as a main dish.*

VARIATION   Add 1 cup chopped or sliced mushrooms.

Tuna Assister

You can't make Tuna Helper either. So make your own Tuna Assister. All you'll do is save money and eliminate additives.

Using the same technique as for Ground Beef Assister (page 116), spread out 1½-foot lengths of waxed paper and prepare mix packages to store in plastic bags.

Tuna 'n' Noodles

On each sheet of paper, mix together:

8 ounces uncooked egg noodles
1 cup instant nonfat dry milk
1 tablespoon unbleached white flour
1 teaspoon paprika
2 teaspoons dried celery leaves
½ teaspoon dry mustard
1 teaspoon salt
⅛ teaspoon ground black pepper

To cook, bring to a boil:

4 cups water

Add:

1 package of mix

Let simmer for 15 minutes. Then add:

1 6½- or 9-ounce can tuna, either oil or water packed

If you use the water packed, add:

a pat of butter

Let simmer, stirring, for 5 more minutes, or until the noodles are done. Serves 4 as a main dish.

Tuna-Cheese Supper

On each sheet of paper, mix together:

8 ounces uncooked macaroni
1 cup instant nonfat dry milk
½ teaspoon thyme
½ teaspoon dillweed
1 teaspoon salt
⅛ teaspoon ground black pepper

To cook, bring to a boil in an oiled frying pan or saucepan:

4 cups water

Add:

1 package of mix

Let simmer, stirring, for 15 minutes. Add:

1 6½- or 9-ounce can tuna   1 cup grated sharp Cheddar
                                     cheese

Let simmer, stirring, for about 5 minutes more, or until the noodles are done. *Serves 4 as a main dish.*

VARIATION   Use grated Italian cheese, Parmesan or Romano, instead of part of the Cheddar.

VARIATIONS ON ALL ASSISTERS USING PASTA   These are real convenience foods that you can prepackage yourself and have on hand. Even the kids can fix a skillet supper without wrecking the kitchen. But use your imagination. A 6½- or 9-ounce can of tuna could be used instead of the beef in the Italian-Style Assister. So could a pound of ground pork sausage, browned and drained, of course. About 1 cup of leftover chopped cooked chicken, beef, or pork would be fine in place of the tuna in either Tuna Assister recipe. The possibilities are endless!

Top-of-the-Stove Stuffing

Here's the way to pay a lot for flavored dried bread—buy it at the store. Here's the way to pay very little for flavored dried bread —make it yourself. For that is all that stuffing mix really is!

Save all of your bits of stale bread before they get moldy. Store a mixture of different kinds in a bag in the freezer. When you get a sizable amount, crumble the bread into ½-inch pieces, spread on a cookie sheet, and put it in the oven just as you turn it off after using it for something else. The idea is to dry out the bread, not cook it. After you dry a batch of bread bits, make your stuffing mix.

Combine:

4 cups dried bread

½ teaspoon garlic powder

¼ cup dried celery leaves

2 tablespoons dried onion
flakes

2 teaspoons dried sweet pepper
flakes

½ teaspoon thyme

½ teaspoon sage

2 teaspoons instant soup
mix (available in jars at
the supermarket under
the Wyler brand or, bet-
ter yet, at health food
stores without MSG un-
der various brand names)
OR 2 bouillon cubes dis-
solved in the boiling
water used to prepare the
stuffing

Because the soup mix and the bouillon cubes may be heavily salted,
add only if needed:

½ teaspoon salt

For convenience, prepare several batches of uncooked stuffing in
advance and store in sealed plastic bags.

To prepare, in a saucepan, combine:

4 cups stuffing mix   1¼ cups boiling water

Stir constantly until the stuffing is moist and fluffy and has absorbed
all of the water. If desired for extra richness, add:

¼ cup Extended Butter (page 211)

To improve the flavor, brown a little under the broiler before serving. Serves 4.

VARIATIONS   Change the seasonings to match your main course.
Add a pinch of rosemary for chicken, marjoram or oregano for beef,
basil for pork. Or add ½ cup sautéed chopped fresh mushrooms.

Chapter 14

Meat Substitutes That Taste Good

WE EAT meat because it is rich in protein. More important, it is rich in the various amino acids that make up *complete* proteins. There are twenty-two amino acids necessary to sustain life. Our bodies can synthesize fourteen of these. There are eight that our bodies *cannot* make. These eight are called *essential amino acids*, and they must all be present at once and in the proper proportions for our bodies to use them. The protein in eggs comes closest to a perfect balance. Thus, we can use over 90 percent of the protein in an egg. We can use about 80 percent of the protein in fish, over 60 percent of that in meat, and over 40 percent of that in peanuts.

However, by mixing various protein-containing foods together, we can increase the useful ratios of the essential amino acids and thereby get more protein for our food dollar.

It is difficult to make the most of complementary proteins every time you fix a meal, of course. But if you keep these basics in mind, you'll do well:

- Milk, cheese, or eggs enhance the protein in just about all meatless dishes.

- A garnish of sesame seeds enhances the protein in most wholegrain dishes.

- Brewer's yeast powder and bran used together enhance the protein in most vegetable dishes.

- Milk improves the protein in potatoes, beans, rice, and corn.

- Soybean powder or flour enhances the protein in wheat.

Meat will always cost more than other protein foods, simply because it takes more land to raise a steer than to grow grains or beans. And with a shrinking and hungry world, eating less meat makes sense, not only in terms of saving money and avoiding dangerous chemicals but as a humanitarian gesture as well.

There is a personal health reason for cutting down on meat, too. Some doctors feel that high meat consumption has a direct bearing on the cholesterol level in our blood and that, in turn, high cholesterol contributes to coronary artery disease. There is also evidence that high meat consumption may be associated with cancer of the colon. So cutting your meat intake is good for you as long as you are careful to get a full range of essential amino acids.

You will find the following recipes for these meat substitutes in this chapter:

Vegetarian Steak

Here's an unusual dish you can make in quantity, freeze, then cook as you need it.

One item at a time, grind in your blender or food processor:

3 cups cooked soybeans

2 cups cooked brown rice

1 large onion

Mix together in a bowl. Then add:

1 cup toasted wheat germ

1 cup cornmeal

3 slightly beaten eggs

1 tablespoon tamari sauce

1 tablespoon salt

1 teaspoon garlic powder

*1 tablespoon brewer's
   yeast powder*

Mix thoroughly and shape into 8 patties. Each of these patties contains about 25 grams of protein, the amount found in 3 ounces of ground lean beef.

Coat a frying pan with:

lecithin pan coating (page 214)

Then add:

1 *tablespoon vegetable oil*

Heat the oil and fry the patties until heated through and golden brown on both sides. Do not turn until the first side is crisp or the patties may fall apart. Top with:

tomato sauce to taste   *grated Parmesan cheese*
                                          to taste

Serves 8.

HINT: If you've never cooked soybeans before, be warned. They take a long time. Soak overnight and cook in a pressure cooker *according to the manufacturer's directions.* This is important because the soybeans can foam, froth, and sputter, clogging up the vent pipe of a pressure cooker. Keep the foam at a safe level by following to the letter the instructions that came with your pressure cooker.

VARIATIONS   You can change the nature of these patties to go with any meal. Top them with cheese and melt under the broiler for a minute or two for additional protein and a different flavor. Or serve with Quick Mushroom Gravy (page 210).

Quiche Lorraine

This is an impressive gourmet dish that will earn you compliments, yet it is a snap to make. In fact, make several ahead of time and freeze them. Here's how:

Line a pie pan with your favorite recipe for:

pastry for a single piecrust

In a frying pan, heat:

1 *tablespoon vegetable oil*

Sauté until it is translucent:

1 *sliced medium onion*

Spread the slices in the bottom of the pie pan, then place the pan in the refrigerator to chill while you make the filling.

To make the filling, place in a blender:

3 *eggs*	½ *teaspoon salt*
¾ *cup milk*	½ *teaspoon thyme*
1 *tablespoon unbleached*	½ *cup sharp Cheddar* OR
white flour	*Colby cheese cubes*

Blend, pour into the chilled piecrust, and dust with:

a little paprika

Bake in a preheated 350-degree oven for about 25 minutes, or until a knife inserted into the center comes out clean.

This is a delicious quiche. The professional secret is the tablespoon of flour in the mix, which prevents the filling from becoming runny. *Makes 6 servings.*

Food Processor Technique

To make the quiche filling in a food processor, place the steel blade in the food processor container. Put in the cheese cubes and process until finely grated. Add the dry ingredients, then, pouring slowly through the chute, add the milk while processing. Finally, add the eggs, one at a time, processing after each is added.

VARIATIONS   Sauté 1 cup sliced fresh mushrooms along with the onion. Or cover the crust with thinly sliced tomatoes, using Swiss cheese instead of or in combination with the Cheddar or Colby.

Main-Dish Vegetable Pancakes

Here's an easy way to fix a delicious high-protein meal. It helps to have a wok, but if you don't, a small frying pan the size of the finished cakes you want will do.

These pancakes may stick during cooking. This is why it helps to use a wok. But with a little practice and by being sure you always keep a small amount of oil in the bottom of the pan, you can quickly get the hang of it.

In a blender, put:

4 eggs
½ cup instant nonfat dry milk
½ cup whole milk
1 onion, cut in quarters
2 ounces Danish blue cheese

2 tablespoons unbleached white flour
2 dashes of Tabasco sauce
1 teaspoon double-acting baking powder
½ teaspoon basil

Blend. Then stir in:

2 cups raw or thawed frozen vegetables—chopped spinach, chopped swiss chard, whole peas, or whatever you wish

Coat a small frying pan or wok with:

lecithin pan coating (page 214)

Add, then heat:

1 tablespoon vegetable oil

Pour in enough of the mixture to make a pancake about ⅜ inch thick. Cook on one side until light brown, then turn and cook on the other side. Continue making cakes, adding an additional tablespoon of oil to the pan for each, until all of the mixture has been cooked. Keep them hot until they are all ready to serve by placing them in a preheated 200-degree oven.

Serve with a sauce if desired. A spicy white sauce with basil and a dash of Tabasco is nice. So is mushroom gravy (see recipe on page 210). *Makes 8 to 10 pancakes.*

VARIATIONS Substitute a good strong Cheddar cheese for the Danish blue. Add 1 tablespoon tamari sauce. Try different sauces.

Macaroni and Cheese

This is an oldie but a goodie. And a great meat substitute. The trouble with macaroni and cheese is that it just isn't a convenience food. Unless you make it this way.

Cook until done, then drain and set aside in the saucepan:

8 ounces uncooked macaroni

Place in a blender:

1½ cups cut-up Cheddar OR
  Colby cheese (about 6
  ounces)
1½ cups milk
1½ tablespoons unbleached
  white flour

1 teaspoon salt
1 tablespoon Extended
  Butter (page 211)
  oil from 1 carrot oil
  capsule

Blend, then pour the mixture over the cooked macaroni. Let simmer over low heat, stirring carefully, for about 5 minutes, or until thickened. Dust the top with:

bread crumbs   paprika

Place under the broiler until crunchy on top. Serve with pride—it tastes so much better than the packaged mix! *Makes 6 servings, or serves 4 as a main dish.*

Food Processor Technique

To make the macaroni and cheese sauce in a food processor, place the steel blade in the food processor container. Put in the cheese pieces and process until finely grated. Add the dry ingredients, then, pouring slowly through the chute, add the milk while processing. Finally, add the butter and carrot oil and process briefly until blended.

Fettucini YOU

When you go to a fancy Italian restaurant, you may sometimes splurge and get Fettucini Alfredo. It is a gourmet dish you probably think you can't get at home. Not so! It is a make-it-yourself convenience food . . . if you know how.

Cook until *al dente* (that means "toothsome," or a bit springy to the tooth), then drain and set aside in the saucepan:

8 ounces uncooked fettucini noodles

Place in a blender:

1 *egg*	2 *tablespoons Extended*
½ *cup whole milk*	*Butter* (page 211)
¼ *cup instant nonfat dry milk*	½ *teaspoon salt*
¼ *cup grated Romano cheese*	½ *teaspoon basil*
(get a good brand or grate	
it yourself—this is what	
makes or breaks this dish)	

Blend thoroughly, then pour the mixture over the cooked noodles. Stir—and keep stirring—over low heat until the noodles are covered with a savory, creamy sauce that would make Alfredo jealous.

Serve at once with a huge salad laced with oil, vinegar, garlic, basil, salt, and pepper. And don't forget a bottle of nice homemade dry white wine (see pages 194–195)! What could be better? *Serves 3 or 4 as a main dish.*

Food Processor Technique

To save money, buy a wedge of good domestic Romano cheese and, using the steel blade, grate it in your food processor before preparing this recipe. Retain ¼ cup of the cheese in the food processor

container. (Store the unused portion in a covered jar in the refrigerator.) Then, put the rest of the sauce ingredients in the container,
cover, and process until smooth. Complete the dish, following the
directions given above.

Chapter 15

Salad Dressings

Fresher Than the Greens

NOTHING is more nutritious than a nice big bowl of fresh greens, topped with a tasty dressing. Right? Wrong! Not when the dressing is laced with monosodium glutamate, sodium alginate, mono-isopropyl citrate, mono- and diglycerides, BHA, BHT, and the rest of the food manufacturer's chemistry set that adds to the shelf life and the cost.

You can make your own salad dressings at home in seconds, at a fraction of the cost of prepared dressing, and actually add to the nutritive value of your salads. If you've been intimidated by salads that talk or leap out of their bowls on TV, or if you are weary of the promises of raves from your guests that appear in the women's magazines, relax. You can do it better yourself.

THE BASIC OIL AND VINEGAR DRESSING

For starters, you need vegetable oil. Buy good oil. It will enhance the flavor of your salad and add to the nutritive value. Here are a few tips:

- Olive oil is fine for salads. It is mono-unsaturated, which means that, while it has no cholesterol, neither does it reduce your cholesterol. It is processed without chemicals.
- Corn oil is a good buy; and if you read the label, you can find a brand in your store that is free of chemicals. If you can't, shop around a bit, because such brands are common.

- Peanut oil is readily available without chemicals. Some people feel, however, that it gives a "peanuty flavor" to delicate foods.
- Stay away from cottonseed oil. Cotton is heavily sprayed for boll weevils, and the oil can contain a residue of pesticides.
- Soybean oil is a bit heavier than corn or safflower oil, but it is readily available with no chemicals.
- Safflower and sunflower oils are the best nutritionally speaking because they are highest in polyunsaturates; they are expensive, but are available without chemicals.
- For nutritive value, switch around somewhat in the varieties of oil you use. Or make a mixture. Corn and olive oil go well together, with the corn oil adding polyunsaturates and the olive oil adding robust flavor. But if you're used to the taste of commercial dressings, start with plain corn oil. You can't go wrong.

Cider vinegar is tasty and the easiest to obtain. Good wine vinegar may be a little trickier to find. Read the label and get a chemical-free brand.

Here are the recipes included in this chapter:

The Absolutely Ideal Salad Dressing

Here is a salad dressing for purists. The only disadvantage is that you can't pour it from a bottle. It is made right on the salad.

Start with a bowl no more than half filled with fresh greens that have been washed and dried. Yes, dried. Toss them in a clean pillowcase. Or line the bowl with paper towels and put the washed, torn greens on the towels, then mop through them with additional towels. But get them dry so that the oil will stick. Then add the other basic ingredients if you are going to use them—tomatoes, onions, sliced peppers, and so on.

Add for each quart of greens:

 2 *tablespoons vegetable oil*

Toss thoroughly to coat all the greens.

Add:

 salt

Easy does it. Too much salt is what spoils most commercial dressings. A light sprinkling is enough.

Add:

 a little ground pepper—freshly ground if possible

If you like garlic, and most people do, now add:

 a sprinkle of powdered garlic

Better yet, rub the bowl with a fresh clove before you put the washed and dried greens into it.

Add:

 herbs to taste

For an Italian meal, use a pinch of basil. For French, a touch of tarragon. Or choose an herb that complements your main course —one that is used in the main-course seasonings, such as sage with poultry, thyme with cheese dishes, or marjoram with steak. Just add a pinch or two.

Stir and toss, mixing thoroughly. Then add:

 2 *teaspoons of apple cider or wine vinegar*

Toss again.

This sounds complicated, but except for washing the greens, which you would do anyway, it takes only a couple of minutes.

And you'll get the best salad dressing your guests ever enjoyed—for a few pennies. Compare this to the sixty cents or so per bottle for additive-loaded commercial dressings.

Homemade Bottled Dressing

To make bottled dressing for more than one salad, take a favorite glass bottle or a covered pint jar, preferably one with a wide mouth so that you can wash out the old oil easily and prevent rancidity.

Measure into it:

¼ cup vinegar
¾ cup vegetable oil
1 teaspoon salt
⅛ teaspoon pepper

¼ teaspoon each garlic powder, basil, dried parsley flakes, mustard seeds

Cover, shake, and allow to sit in the refrigerator for an hour or so for the flavor to develop. Shake or stir before each use. *Makes 1 cup.*

VARIATION   People who go to steak houses love the creamy Italian dressing. Make your own by using the basic homemade bottled dressing recipe, putting it into a blender, adding 1 teaspoon liquid lecithin, and whipping it for a few seconds until it is smooth and creamy.

French Dressing

Some of the bottled pink and orange goop that passes for "French" dressing could cause an international incident if the people in France ever tasted the vile mixtures attributed to them. Actually, the traditional French dressing is delicious if properly made. And nothing is easier.

Put in a blender or shaker jar:

⅓ cup vinegar
⅔ cup vegetable oil
½ teaspoon dry mustard
½ teaspoon salt

½ teaspoon paprika
dash of Tabasco sauce
1 teaspoon liquid lecithin

Blend or shake until smooth and creamy. *Makes 1 cup.*

Oil-Free Blue Cheese Dressing

If you like rich, creamy blue cheese dressing, but would like to eliminate the calories that vegetable oil adds to salad dressing, make this oil-free variety.

Put into a blender:

1 cup homemade yogurt (see pages 59–60)
2 teaspoons vinegar

2 ounces Danish blue cheese (good Danish blue cheese lacks the bleaching agents and chemicals of some blue cheeses)

Mix, serve, and enjoy. *Makes about 1¼ cups.*

Tomato-Blue Cheese Dressing

This is a tangy dressing that really sets off a hearty steak dinner.

In a jar, combine:

1 cup tomato juice OR mixed vegetable juice
2 ounces crumbled Danish blue cheese
2 teaspoons vinegar

2 tablespoons vegetable oil (optional)
dash of Tabasco sauce
pinch of basil

Shake and serve. *Makes about 1½ cups.*

Super-Delicious Blender Mayonnaise

It is impossible to give a recipe for blender mayonnaise with precise measurements for ingredients. Strange things affect the magic! But with a little practice and a little courage, you can make homemade mayonnaise that tastes better than any you can buy in a store. And it's less expensive, too.

First, a little theory. Mayonnaise is an *emulsion*. Oil and water, as you know, won't mix. But in mayonnaise, oil and vinegar (which is basically water) do mix and stay mixed through the action of an *emulsifier*. Lecithin, which you can read about on page 21, is a natural emulsifier. Egg yolks are rich in lecithin. Therefore, by mixing egg yolks, water, and oil in the right proportions, you can get an emulsion—and, properly flavored, this emulsion is called mayonnaise.

Unfortunately, nature doesn't always cooperate with theory. So you do best with mayonnaise when you help it along. Here's how.

Start by chilling your blender container and your vegetable oil. Select a fairly heavy oil. Corn oil is excellent. Safflower oil, which is very light, is tricky to work with.

In your clean, cold container, whip:

2 egg yolks	¼ to ½ teaspoon salt (to
1 teaspoon liquid lecithin	taste)
½ teaspoon dry mustard	2 tablespoons vinegar

Here's the tricky part. While the mixture is whipping, remove the cover and *slowly* trickle in the cold oil. This two-egg-yolk mayonnaise will absorb about:

1½ cups vegetable oil

and will yield approximately 2 cups of mayonnaise. If necessary during this process, increase the speed of your blender a bit as the mixture thickens. Suddenly, your mixture will "set," and you will have mayonnaise!

Now, here is the secret of the light, fluffy texture of commercial mayonnaise. Using a rubber spatula to carefully scrape the sides of your blender, slowly add:

up to 2 tablespoons cold water

until the mayonnaise reaches the desired consistency. Scrape the mayonnaise into a clean jar, cover, and refrigerate. That's all there is to it—*except* . . .

If, while you are pouring in the oil, the mixture suddenly looks thin and curdly, stop, pour the mixture into another container, then put into the blender and whip:

1 whole egg

Then, with the blender running, drizzle the mixture from the reserve container into the egg. Mayonnaise *always* takes on the second time around! Then, if you wish, you can add a little water, though you will find the added egg white has given the mayonnaise a fluffier texture. *Makes about 2 cups.*

VARIATIONS   To make a delicious topping to serve over sliced cucumbers, mix ¼ teaspoon dillweed with ½ cup mayonnaise. Or, as a topping for fish, try ¼ teaspoon curry powder mixed with ½ cup mayonnaise. Fish is also good served with tartar sauce made by combining 2 tablespoons drained pickle relish and 1 tablespoon finely chopped onion with ½ cup mayonnaise.

Food Processor Mayonnaise

Making mayonnaise in a food processor is much less tricky than making it in a blender. In fact, it's practically fail-proof. Here is a recipe for a whole-egg mayonnaise that doesn't require liquid lecithin or water. The egg whites give it a light, fluffy texture and add nutritive value.

Place the plastic or steel blade in the processor. In the container, put:

2 *egg yolks*	¼ *to* ½ *teaspoon salt (to taste)*
½ *teaspoon dry mustard*	2 *tablespoons vinegar*

Turn on the processor and whip briefly. Then, with the processor running, slowly pour through the chute:

1½ *cups vegetable oil*

Turn the processor off and add both at once:

2 *egg whites*

Process again just until thoroughly blended through. Scoop into a clean jar, cover, and refrigerate. *Makes about 2 cups.*

Cole Slaw and Potato Salad Dressing

In a small bowl, combine and stir together:

½ *cup homemade mayonnaise*	1 *teaspoon sugar*
(see page 135)	*scant* ¼ *teaspoon*
½ *cup plain yogurt*	*dillweed (optional)*
2 *teaspoons vinegar*	½ *teaspoon garlic powder*

Salad ingredients may include shredded green or red cabbage for cole slaw, or sliced cooked potatoes, combined with chopped raw onion, celery, and green pepper. Salt and pepper the salad to taste, add enough dressing to make it quite moist, stir it through gently, pour it into a serving bowl, and sprinkle the top with paprika. *Makes 1 cup dressing, or enough for 4 cups cole slaw or potato salad.*

VARIATION   This dressing is also delicious with alfalfa sprouts substituted for shredded cabbage in the cole slaw.

Yogurt Fruit Salad Dressing

In a small bowl, combine and stir together:

1 *cup plain yogurt*	1 *teaspoon honey*
¼ *cup fruit juice from a fruit to be used in the salad*	

Spoon the dressing over individual fruit salads just before serving. If desired, top each serving with a small cube of cream cheese garnished with half a walnut or pecan. A scoop of cottage cheese also makes a delicious and nutritious accompaniment. *Makes 1¼ cups of dressing.*

Salad Toppings

Here is a list of several delicious foods to top off your favorite vegetable salads. They provide a good way to use small amounts of leftovers.

homemade croutons   *crumbled hard-cooked eggs*
cooked chick-peas   *leftover cooked and*
crumbled or slivered cheese   *slivered chicken or beef*

Chapter 16

Sweets That Are All Natural

IF FOOD COSTS bother you, consider this. The wholesale price of sugar is about 10¢ per pound. The cost of a candy bar at the store is anywhere from $1.00 a pound up to over $2.50 a pound. Isn't that a lot to pay for processing, packaging, and cavities for the kids?

Saccharin causes cancer and will undoubtedly be banned.

Sugar—refined, white, "pure" sugar—is being denounced more and more by experts in medicine and nutrition. It is suspect in cases of high cholesterol, obesity, hypoglycemia, and many of the other ills that beset our times. But . . . if you *must* eat sweets, you may as well save yourself the money and use plain white sugar in their preparation. Raw sugar, nutritionally, is so little better that it's not worth the extra cost. Honey is your best bet, however. It is about half fructose, or fruit sugar, which is superior to white sugar (sucrose). Because fructose is twice as sweet as sucrose, you can use less and thereby cut some calories from your diet. You and your family can learn to like it if you don't already. Try different varieties. Many people who don't care too much for honey find that they like the interesting flavor of buckwheat honey, for example.

As with other items, you can make your own sweet foods. You can cut costs, make a carob bar that is far superior to chocolate bars nutritionally, for about seventy-five cents as opposed to the one dollar or more you'd pay for the commercial candy. Here are the recipes you'll find in this chapter:

CANDY

Fruit Jellies

Here's an easy-to-make candy you can fix at home. Use the powdered pectin available in your store under the Sure-Jell label. It is relatively free of chemicals.

In a saucepan, mix together:

2 1¾-ounce boxes powdered
   pectin
¾ cup water

1 6-ounce can frozen or-
   ange juice concentrate,
   thawed
1 teaspoon baking soda

In a 4-quart saucepan, mix together:

2 *cups sugar*   1 *teaspoon vanilla*
1⅓ *cups light corn syrup*

Bring the contents of both pans to a rapid boil and cook, stirring, for 6 to 8 minutes. Next, pour the pectin-juice mixture slowly into the sugar pan, stirring continuously. Bring to a boil again and stir constantly as it cooks for 1 more minute.

Remove from the heat, let sit for 1 minute, still stirring, then pour into two 10-by-5-by-1-inch aluminum foil pans coated with:

lecithin pan coating (page 214)

Set aside, uncovered, until cooled and firm, about 3 hours.

The only tricky part about making this candy is unmolding it and cutting it into edible pieces. It is extremely sticky until it is coated with sugar. With a sharp-pointed knife, gently cut all around the top edges of one of the pans, separating the bond that has formed between the pan and the top of the candy. Then, gently pull the sides of the flexible pan away from the candy and invert it on a sheet of aluminum foil. Remove the pan, peeling away the candy if necessary. Repeat with the second pan. Into a flat bowl, put:

½ *cup granulated sugar*

Using a sharp pizza cutter, cut the candy into 1-inch squares. Peel the pieces of candy from the foil and place several at a time in the bowl of sugar. Spoon the sugar over the pieces of candy until each is coated. After all of the squares of candy have been sugar coated, spread them out, uncovered and not touching, on waxed paper to sit overnight in a dry place. Then store in a flat cardboard box with waxed paper between the layers. *Makes 2 pounds or about 80 pieces.*

VARIATIONS   Try different fruit juices for different flavors. Grape, cranberry, apple, or lemonade juice concentrates may be used.

Carob Bars

Have you checked the price of chocolate bars lately? You might also check the nutritional differences between carob and chocolate: There is no allergic reaction to carob. Carob has less than half the calories of chocolate. Chocolate contains theobromine, a relative of caffeine that is very undesirable.

Chocolate bars are basically a fat product, sweetened with sugar, emulsified to allow the two bases to mix, then flavored with chocolate and other ingredients. Here's how to make your own substitute.

In a saucepan, melt:

1½ sticks (¾ cup) margarine

Do NOT use the polyunsaturated or liquid type. You want a margarine that will solidify at room temperature. Slowly add, in order, stirring constantly while the mixture simmers:

1 tablespoon liquid lecithin   *½ cup instant nonfat dry*
1 cup confectioner's sugar   *milk*
½ cup powdered carob

When thoroughly mixed, add:

1 teaspoon pure vanilla extract

Then, while still hot, pour into a blender and whip for a few seconds. Pour into a 10-by-5-by-1-inch aluminum foil pan. Cool, uncovered, in the refrigerator for several hours, or until firm. Pull away the flexible sides of the pan from the candy and unmold the bar onto a sheet of aluminum foil large enough to wrap it. Store in the refrigerator because it contains no preservatives. To serve, cut into smaller bars or break off bite-sized pieces. *Makes 12 ounces or 6 2-ounce bars.*

You'll love it! But remember, it's fattening. And the sugar still causes cavities, even if it is in a make-your-own-foods candy.

VARIATIONS   Add ½ teaspoon or more pure peppermint extract. Or stir in 1 cup coconut or roasted peanuts or other nuts as you mold the candy.

Lion's Milk Bars

If you think regular candy is expensive, try health food store candy! Here's the way to make your own version of a popular favorite.

In a bowl, stir together:

¾ cup peanut butter	2 tablespoons sugar
1 tablespoon brewer's yeast powder	1 cup instant nonfat dry milk

Work until thoroughly mixed. This is a dry mixture, so it won't be easy to do. Or combine the ingredients more quickly in a food processor.

Shape into small bars. Dip them into:

2 small melted commercial carob bars (the kind you buy at the health food store)

Coat completely, and let dry on waxed paper. Store, wrapped, in the refrigerator because they contain no preservatives. *Makes 6 2-ounce bars.*

NOTE: If the carob bars are difficult to melt, add:

1 teaspoon vegetable oil

VARIATIONS   Add coconut, raisins, or chopped pitted dates or nuts.

Best-Yet Candy

Here's an old-fashioned, easy-to-make confection that is especially popular at Thanksgiving and Christmas.

Stuff:

pitted dates

with

whole almonds OR walnut pieces OR peanut butter

Roll in:

sugar OR *shredded coconut*

Serve.

Store, covered, in the refrigerator because they contain no preservatives.

Instant Candy

Here's a fast and tasty candy. But it still has lots of calories!

Health food stores sell marvelous, very sweet dried pineapple slices. For the fastest candy on record, cut into 8 sections each:

slices dried pineapple

Wrap and store in a dry place.

VARIATION Dip the sections into melted commercial carob bars and dry on waxed paper.

Fruit and Nut Balls

In a blender or food processor, separately grind the following ingredients, emptying each into a bowl:

½ *cup raw almonds* OR *walnuts*	1 *pound chopped pitted dates*
½ *cup shredded coconut*	1 *cup raisins*

Add:

1 *teaspoon honey*	1 *teaspoon pure vanilla extract*

Mix together well or whip together in the food processor. Shape into small balls and roll in:

additional shredded coconut

Chill in the refrigerator until ready to serve. Store, covered, in the refrigerator. *Makes 4 to 5 dozen balls.*

VARIATIONS   Instead of rolling in coconut, dip the balls into melted commercial carob bars and dry on waxed paper.

FROZEN DESSERTS AND SNACKS

Quick Carob Ice Cream

In a blender, mix:

1 14-ounce can condensed (not   1 teaspoon pure vanilla
   evaporated) milk   extract
¼ cup powdered carob   1 cup milk

Pour into a bowl, cover, and freeze for 3 to 4 hours. *Makes 4 servings.*

VARIATION   For vanilla ice cream, omit the carob and substitute ¼ cup instant nonfat dry milk.

Frozen Yogurt

Here's a delicious version of this newly popular food.

In a blender, put:

¼ cup boiling water   1 envelope unflavored gelatin

Blend to dissolve. Add:

3 cups plain homemade yogurt   1 teaspoon pure vanilla
   (see pages 59–60)   extract
1 10-ounce package frozen
   sweetened strawberries,
   thawed

Blend briefly. Cover and freeze. If you have a churn-type ice-cream freezer, fine. Otherwise, freeze for about 2 hours, until it is beginning to firm, then whip quickly with an electric mixer until smooth. Freeze again for about 2 more hours before serving. Serve soft like commercial frozen custard. *Makes a little over 1 quart.*

VARIATIONS Substitute 10 ounces of any fresh, canned, or frozen fruit for the strawberries, and sweeten to taste.

The Fastest Snack Ever

Peel:

several ripe bananas

Wrap them separately in plastic wrap. Freeze overnight. Unwrap and eat frozen.

HINT: Don't plan to store these in your freezer for more than a week, because they will become dark and watery.

VARIATION Plan to freeze a bunch. Dip banana halves into melted commercial carob bars, then let them dry, not touching, on a cookie sheet. Wrap and freeze. If desired, these can be skewered on wooden Popsicle sticks before dipping and freezing for less messy eating.

JELLY

Grape Jelly

You can make your own grape jelly easily and inexpensively in minutes.

In a saucepan, mix:

1 6-ounce can frozen unsweet-ened grape juice concentrate

2½ cups water

1 box powdered pectin (Sure-Jell is recommended)

Bring to a boil. Add:

3¾ cups sugar

Boil hard for 1 minute, stirring constantly. Skim if needed and pour into small sterile jars. Cover with paraffin. Better still, pour into small sterile jars with two-piece lids. Put the lids tightly on the jars. Invert briefly, then seal. Store in a cool, dry place. *Makes 4 8-ounce jars.*

VARIATIONS Substitute other juice concentrates for the grape. Note that the grape juice concentrate has no added sugar. Other juices may or may not. For those that do, reduce the sugar added by about ¼ cup.

PUDDINGS

Pasha

This is a healthful and absolutely delicious dessert.

In a blender or food processor, put:

1 *pound cottage cheese*	2 *tablespoons milk*
¼ *cup sugar*	1 *teaspoon pure vanilla*
1 *tablespoon softened*	*extract*
Extended Butter (page 211)	

Blend until smooth and creamy. Pour into a colander lined with a clean cloth or a double layer of cheesecloth. Fold the cloth ends over the top and weight down with a small plate. Sit the colander in a pie pan in the refrigerator and allow the excess liquid to drain off overnight.

Serve cold with a topping of fruit or preserves or a sprinkle of granola or toasted coconut. Or use this as a topping for fruit or as a sweet spread for toast or cookies. *Makes 3 ½-cup servings.*

Carob Pudding

In a blender, mix:

⅓ cup sugar	2 tablespoons Extended
¼ cup cornstarch	Butter (see page 211)
¼ cup powdered carob	1 teaspoon pure vanilla
2¾ cups milk	extract

Blend. Pour into a saucepan that has been coated with:

lecithin pan coating (page 214)

Heat slowly, stirring constantly. Then boil for 1 minute, stirring constantly. Cool slightly, then pour back into the blender and whip again. Pour into serving dishes. Chill in the refrigerator for several hours. *Serves 6.*

VARIATIONS   Reduce the milk by ¼ cup and substitute ¼ cup bourbon or rum. Or make vanilla pudding by omitting the carob and adding 1 more teaspoon pure vanilla extract.

Whipped Topping

If you don't want the price or cholesterol of heavy cream, the cost of instant whipped cream, or the chemicals in the ersatz topping, this is the stuff for you.

Get out your trusty box of instant nonfat dry milk. And put your small electric mixer bowl and beaters in the freezer for a little while. When they are good and chilled, whip until it forms peaks:

½ cup instant nonfat dry milk   ½ cup ice water

This takes 3 to 4 minutes. Add:

2 tablespoons lemon juice

and whip for another 3 to 4 minutes, or until stiff. If you want it sweet, fold in up to:

1/4 cup sugar   1 teaspoon pure vanilla extract

and serve at once. This has a mild citrus flavor and is good on gelatin or fruit desserts. *It makes about 3½ cups.*

VARIATION   Use iced fruit juice instead of water; this will add interesting color and flavor to your topping.

PIES AND CAKE

Carob Pie

Make:

>   *one-half of the recipe for Carob Pudding* (see opposite page)

adding:

>   *½ envelope unflavored gelatin dissolved in 2 tablespoons boiling water*

during the last blender whipping. Pour into:

>   *a baked, flaky piecrust*

and chill for several hours, or until set. If desired, top individual servings with:

>   *a dollop of unsweetened whipped cream*

Makes 6 servings.

VARIATIONS   Use the variations suggested for Carob Pudding.

Pasha Pie

A day ahead of the time you wish to serve this, make:

>   *Pasha* (page 147)

The following day, after the Pasha has drained, mix it thoroughly with:

1 envelope of unflavored gelatin dissolved in ¼ cup boiling water

Fill:

a baked, flaky piecrust

and chill for several hours or until set. *Serves 6.*

VARIATION   This is great with a graham cracker crust or topped with sweetened pineapple that has been thickened with cornstarch.

To make the topping, stir together:

2 tablespoons sugar   1 tablespoon cornstarch

Adding a little at a time, gradually dissolve the sugar-cornstarch mixture in:

1 8-ounce can unsweetened crushed pineapple

Cook over medium heat, stirring constantly, until the mixture becomes thick and clear. Cool to room temperature, then spread over the chilled, set pie.

Lemon Pie

Here's an old favorite that the makers of condensed milk (condensed, not evaporated) are quite understandably proud of. It works because lemon juice reacts with and stiffens the condensed milk.

In a bowl, whip together with a spoon until smooth and creamy:

1 14-ounce can condensed   2 slightly beaten egg yolks
milk   juice of 2 lemons

Pour into:

a graham cracker crust

and chill for several hours, or until set. Period. If desired, top individual servings with:

a dollop of unsweetened whipped cream OR *Whipped Topping* (page 148)

This is very rich, so small servings will do. *Makes 6 to 8 servings.*

Yogurt Loaf Cake

What are convenient make-your-own foods without a cake mix? Here's a simple one you can make on the spot, or store the premixed dry ingredients in plastic bags, ready to go at a moment's notice.

In a bowl, mix together:

1¾ *cups unbleached white flour*	1 *teaspoon double-acting*
3 *tablespoons cornstarch*	*baking powder*
¾ *cup sugar*	¾ *teaspoon soda*
	½ *teaspoon salt*

In a blender, whip together:

1 *cup plain yogurt made with reconstituted milk* (see page 60) (*a very tart yogurt is required here*)	½ *cup Extended Butter* (page 211)
	2 *eggs*
	2 *teaspoons pure vanilla extract*

Add the dry ingredients. Blend again until just mixed, scraping down the sides of the blender. If your blender has trouble mixing this, empty the ingredients into a bowl and mix thoroughly with a spoon.

Pour into a standard loaf pan coated with:

lecithin pan coating (page 214)

or greased and lined on the bottom with waxed paper. Bake in a preheated 350-degree oven for about 50 minutes. Cool on a rack for 15 minutes before removing the cake from the pan. *Makes 8 generous servings.*

Food Processor Technique

Place the steel blade in the food processor. First, evenly distribute the dry ingredients in the processor container. Next, cut the butter into 3 or 4 pieces and evenly distribute them in the container. Finally, add the yogurt, eggs, and vanilla. Process for a few seconds until the ingredients are well blended. Scrape down the sides of the container. Process again, for 1 minute. Scrape down the sides of the container again. Process for ½ minute more. Pour the batter into a prepared loaf pan and bake as described above.

Electric Mixer Technique

Cakes made with an electric mixer tend to have a smoother texture than those prepared with high-speed blenders or food processors. If you prefer to make this cake with an electric mixer, here are the directions. Place the Extended Butter (it should be at room temperature) in the large mixer bowl, add all of the dry ingredients and two-thirds of the yogurt mixed with the vanilla. Mix at moderate speed for 2 minutes. Add the rest of the yogurt and the eggs and mix for 1 minute more. Pour the batter into a prepared loaf pan and bake as described above.

VARIATIONS   For carob cake, cut the flour by ½ cup and substitute ½ cup powdered carob.

For spice cake, to the dry ingredients add: 1 teaspoon ground cinnamon, ½ teaspoon nutmeg, ½ teaspoon allspice, and ½ teaspoon ground ginger.

Fast and Creamy Icing

In your blender or food processor, put:

1 cup confectioner's sugar	¼ cup room-temperature
1 tablespoon cottage cheese	butter or margarine (not
	Extended Butter)
	½ teaspoon pure vanilla extract

Blend until smooth, scraping down the sides of the container from time to time. *Makes enough to ice the top of 1 loaf cake.*

VARIATION   For a creamy carob-flavored icing, add 1 tablespoon carob powder and blend along with the other ingredients.

COOKIES

Swedish Refrigerator Cookies

Here's a quick and easy recipe for making your own food-processor slice-and-bake cookies. If you wish, you can make the dough in advance, freeze it, then thaw, slice, and bake the cookies as needed.

Place the steel blade in the food processor. Then put in the container, in the order given:

2 cups unbleached white flour
½ cup sugar
1 cup Extended Butter (see page 211), cut into several chunks and distributed evenly in the container

1 egg
1 teaspoon pure vanilla extract

Place the lid on the container and process until the stiff dough forms a ball. Take the dough out of the container and shape it into 2 rolls about 1¼ inches in diameter. Wrap them in waxed paper and chill overnight. Using a sharp knife, cut into thin slices and bake in a preheated 400-degree oven for about 8 or 9 minutes, or until they are golden brown around the edges. *Makes about 7 dozen small cookies.*

Granola Cookies

You can buy granola cookies—if you can afford them! Or, of course, you can make your own.

In a blender, put:

1 egg
½ cup Extended Butter (page 211)

1 teaspoon pure vanilla extract

Blend together until well mixed.

In a bowl, mix together:

¾ cup unbleached white flour
1 cup sugar
1½ cups homemade granola cereal (see pages 49–50)

½ teaspoon baking soda
½ teaspoon salt

Stir in the butter-egg mixture. Drop by teaspoonfuls onto cookie sheets and bake in a preheated 350-degree oven for about 10 or 12 minutes, or until golden brown. *Makes about 4 dozen cookies.*

HINT: The dry ingredients for this recipe could be premeasured, mixed, and stored away in packages like cookie mix. Adding the moist ingredients and baking when freshly made cookies are wanted would then be a simple, quick process.

Carob–Sunflower Seed Cookies

In a blender, put:

2 eggs
⅔ cup corn oil

2 teaspoons pure vanilla extract

Blend together until well mixed.

In a bowl, mix together:

1½ cups unbleached white flour
½ cup raw wheat germ
½ cup raw sunflower seeds
¼ cup powdered carob

¾ cup sugar
2 teaspoons double-acting baking powder
½ teaspoon salt

Stir in the oil-egg mixture and mix well. Drop onto cookie sheets by the teaspoonful. Bake in a preheated 350-degree oven for 8 to 10 minutes. *Makes approximately 4 dozen cookies.*

HINT: The dry ingredients for this recipe could be premeasured, mixed, and stored away in packages like cookie mix. Adding the moist ingredients and baking when freshly made cookies are wanted would then be a simple, quick process.

Chapter 17

Easy and Inexpensive Baby Foods

IN THE OLD DAYS, it is said, some Jewish parents would give their child a book with a small dab of honey on the cover. The child would taste the sweet honey and make an immediate association, that is, honey is sweet, therefore learning is sweet. This was a charming custom that no doubt enhanced learning—and a tendency toward diabetes.

Fact: Many top nutritionists agree that the two most common dangerous additives in our food are sugar and salt. Second fact: We teach our kids to love both these seasonings. And they are seasonings, not food, because natural sweets and salts abound in common foods; and man could very well do without extra amounts of either one.

Dr. Carlton Fredericks, an outstanding nutritionist, recently reported an interview he had with an executive of a baby-foods company. This company, be it noted, has been a leader in cutting down on salt and sugar in baby foods. After all, the salt and sugar is only put there so that mommy will think it tastes good when she licks the spoon! Anyway, this executive was bragging that in some of their foods, the sugar content had been reduced to 9 percent. Pretty good, huh? Doesn't sound like much at all, does it? But consider, as Dr. Fredericks points out, that 9 percent sugar is the equivalent of *five*, count 'em, *five* teaspoons of sugar in a cup of coffee!

What would happen if our kids grew up without the desire for salt and sugar that we build into them? To quote Dr. Fredericks, "If we succeed in arriving at a generation of babies in whom we have not fanned the desire for sugar and salt, we may make significant inroads on the incidence of tooth decay, diabetes, hypoglycemia, high blood pressure and numerous other degenerative diseases."

That's the nutrition side of the picture. Or part of it at least. Then there's the cost side. It does seem a shame to pay high prices for neat little jars of baby food when you feed the nutritious extras from your own meals to the family pet. Junior deserves as good a shot at things as Rover.

You can make your own baby foods, even though the big companies spend a lot of money to convince you that you can't. And yours will be fresher. And you'll know just what is, and isn't, in them. Here are a few simple, basic tips:

- Use equipment that is spotlessly clean.
- Don't store uneaten food for long periods. How many mothers open a can of commercial baby food, sterile before the seal was broken, feed baby a bit, dipping back and forth into the jar, then store it in the refrigerator for a few days? The bacteria from the baby's mouth could be setting up a great germ culture. The danger is just as great with homemade food.
- If you make extra food, freeze it at once until needed.
- If you feed the baby from food prepared for the family, take out his portion before adding any seasonings. Drastically reduce the amounts of sugar and salt you would normally use.
- Cook fruits and vegetables in the smallest amount of water possible, as quickly as possible. A pressure cooker is great.
- Be careful to eliminate bits of bone, skin, gristle, and fat from meats.
- Homemade soups make great baby foods, but, again, remove the baby's serving before adding seasonings.
- Whip the food in a blender or food processor to the desired consistency, keeping the baby's age and chewing ability in mind. Some blender manufacturers sell small jars with lids in which food can be blended, then stored. Or there are even inexpensive hand grinders available, from which you can feed directly.

· To get variety, prepare a quantity of food—say, half a blender container—and freeze it in an ice cube tray. Pop out the frozen food cubes into a plastic bag and label. Thaw required amounts as needed in the refrigerator, then warm them slightly before serving.

WHAT TO FEED BABY

Try these basic suggestions.

Yogurt

Babies usually love yogurt. And it is easy to digest. Just use the plain, homemade variety (see pages 59–60). For kids who have trouble digesting plain milk, especially, yogurt can be the answer.

Yogurt is also good mixed with cereals or fruits. If you must sweeten it, use a small dab of honey.

Fruit Pasha

Here's a delicious food that's a snap to make.

Just blend together:

1 *cup cottage cheese*	1 *cup fresh* OR *canned* OR *frozen fruit*

If you gotta, add 1 teaspoon honey.

Pureed Meats

To get a smooth blended product, you may need a favorite secret ingredient used by food manufacturers—water. Put in a blender or food processor cooked meat of any kind (except ham or bacon, which contains dangerous nitrates and nitrites) or cooked fish (watch out for tiny bones). Grind until the meat is finely chopped, then add a little water and blend again until the meat purees.

VARIATIONS   Add cooked rice and/or vegetables.

Vegetables

Simplicity, simplicity! Just blend cooked, unseasoned vegetables in a small amount of their own juice until you have a smooth puree, junior-sized chunks, or whatever you wish.

Fruits

Even more simple! Blend a ripe banana (ripe is more digestible). Period.

Or, if you wish, quickly cook peeled apples, or peaches or plums in a small amount of water and blend.

DON'TS

Don't feed small infants corn or popcorn, nuts, raw carrots, raw onions, cooked dried beans.

FOR OLDER KIDS...

You know when the baby is ready for finger foods. Or better yet, ask your doctor. Then you can feed him or her:

strips of soft cheese	*strawberries*
sliced hard-cooked eggs	*cantaloupe pieces*
carrot sticks	*whole bananas*
peeled tomatoes	*small meatballs*
cooked asparagus tips	*chicken slices*
cooked broccoli flowerets	*toast, either buttered or*
cooked string beans	*plain*
peeled apple quarters	*homemade cookies*
peeled, seeded orange	*homemade breads*
sections	*cold cereals*

The list could go on and on. Add to it yourself!

FOR STILL OLDER KIDS...

Recipes aren't as important as principles:

- Teach the kids to avoid junk foods. They really *can* grow up without unhealthful, store-bought snacks.
- Define junk foods for them by example and in fact as they grow older. Junk foods are filled with empty calories in the form of sugar and have few nutrients. Pizza isn't a junk food; neither is a cheeseburger. Soft drinks and candy bars are. So teach them to like and want a hamburger or tuna sandwich and milk instead of salty french fries and a chocolate sundae.

Chapter 18

Safe and Convenient

Brown-Bag Lunches

TAKE a few minutes and meet some unpleasant bugs.

First, there's *salmonella*. This ugly little guy causes fever, nausea, vomiting, and diarrhea.

Then there's *staphylococcus* or, as those who know and hate it call it, *staph*. It is probably the most common germ in existence. As a contaminant in food, it causes stomach pains, nausea, vomiting, and diarrhea.

Next there's *coliform bacillus*, a totally unpleasant bug that causes symptoms similar to the ones listed above.

Finally, there's the dreaded *Clostridium botulinum*, which causes botulism, a frequently fatal form of food poisoning.

Where do these germs come from? And how do they spread illness?

First of all, realize that bacteria reproduce by fission, that is, by the simple device of each cell splitting into two cells. Thus, under favorable conditions, a single germ cell, splitting every half hour, will, by the end of fifteen hours, have created a colony of 1 *billion* cells.

So the trick is to keep bacteria out of food in the first place. Since that is impossible to do completely, the second preventive step is to make conditions for bacterial growth as unfavorable as possible.

Germs come from common sources. Salmonella can come from contamination by rats, mice, flies, birds, and humans. It is most often found in luncheon meats, pies, creamy foods, ice cream, breads, and cakes. The symptoms of salmonella poisoning start about twelve hours after the contaminated food is eaten. It can easily be prevented by carefully washing the hands after using the toilet and before eating and by keeping food refrigerated and away from insects and rodents. Don't buy from suspicious sources! Thorough cooking destroys salmonella.

Staph itself is not poisonous. The toxins the bacteria exude are, and they *cannot be destroyed by heat.* So the contamination must be stopped before it ever starts. Eat fresh food; be especially careful of ham, cold cuts, and milk products. Don't handle food if you have an open or infected cut.

Coliform bacteria are common in the intestinal tracts of humans and animals, so again, the rule is to wash thoroughly after using the toilet and before eating.

Finally, botulism is the most dangerous of the food poisonings, but the least common. The bacteria grow everywhere, but they are harmless. Like staph, it is the exuded toxin that is harmful; but, in the case of botulism, thorough cooking destroys the toxin. It usually occurs in improperly canned foods, such as those prepared at home with improper equipment, so that the can of food itself is an ideal place for the bacteria to grow. If a can looks suspicious, that is, if it bulges or is off-color, don't taste it. It only takes a drop to get you! Throw it away! And cook home-canned foods at a boil for fifteen minutes just for safety.

What has all of this to do with brown-bag lunches? Just this. With restaurant prices going up, brown-bagging-it makes a lot of sense. But. When certain foods sit in a warm spot from the time the lunch was prepared until it is eaten, it gives ample time for a culture of harmful bacteria to grow and keep you home the next day with a mysterious "virus." So follow these tips for brown-bagging-it and you'll be safe. And don't assume that by eating in a restaurant you'll absolutely avoid food poisoning either. Be careful and trust yourself, and you can be just as safe or safer with that brown-bag lunch!

START WITH BEING CLEAN

Keep yourself and the food clean, and you'll eliminate a lot of food poisoning problems.

· Keep flies away from food.
· Don't handle food if you have cuts or any kind of infection on your hands.
· Use a separate cutting board for raw meat. Scrub it thoroughly between uses.
· Don't use the same plate or wrap for cooked meat as you did for the raw—raw meat contains bacteria.
· Wash carefully after handling pets, using the toilet, before handling food.
· Keep work areas and utensils clean. If possible, work on waxed paper.

KEEP HOT FOODS HOT

Any food left at room temperature for more than 2 hours is a possible source of food poisoning. So if a food should be eaten hot, keep it hot.

· Buy and use a good thermos bottle for hot milk drinks and soups.

KEEP COLD FOODS COLD

If food is kept below 40 degrees Fahrenheit, germs don't grow very well. So keep brown-bag foods cold. Here's how.

· For vegetable salads, store in an insulated bag with a refreezable ice cannister next to the salad container.
· Do the same for fruit pies.
· For sandwiches, stick to less perishable items such as meat or cheese, then freeze the sandwich the night before. Pack it

frozen. By lunchtime it will be thawed, fresh, and, above all, safe. Do not use mayonnaise on frozen sandwiches because it will separate and ruin the food; do not freeze lettuce or tomatoes because they will turn mushy. Mustard and catsup are fine as condiments.

- Pack chilled fruit as a refreshing brown-bag extra. Be sure it is clean. And don't forget whole tomatoes.
- Hard-cooked eggs, unpeeled and wrapped, keep well.
- If your office or shop has a refrigerator for employee lunches, use it.
- Don't store your waiting lunch in a warm place, such as near a radiator, in a closed locker, or on a windowsill.
- Be sure any meat is well done and fresh.
- Buy a lunch box. They're easy to keep clean, and they act as good insulators.
- Don't try to save leftovers. Pack just as much as you can eat.

IDEAS

These foods are convenient to fix and keep well:

- Meat and cheese sandwiches.
- Meat loaf or cold roast beef sandwiches.
- Plain cheese sandwiches, any kind.
- Peanut butter sandwiches.
- Chef's salads. Pack the lettuce in a plastic bowl on ice. Add the meat, cheese, tomato, hard-cooked egg, and dressing just before eating. Keep cold!
- Cookies, crackers, or any kind of dried foods.

WHAT TO AVOID

- Anything with mayonnaise, especially tuna, chicken, or potato salads.

- Creamy dressings or desserts.
- Don't pack milk; buy it fresh where you work or keep a supply there in the refrigerator.
- Anything that spoils easily.

There is an old adage among health food nuts. "Don't eat anything that won't spoil, but eat it before it does." That's good advice. And it's never more true than in the case of brown-bag lunches!

Chapter 19

Frozen Dinners

You'll Be Proud to Serve

Can you really picture serving a TV dinner to company? The pasty mashed potatoes; the stringy, scanty portion of meat; the bullet-like peas; the "dessert," into which the salty gravy overflowed? TV dinners are not a tribute to American culinary skills.

Nor are they a bargain. The cost per pound of protein is astronomical. The old adage, "You get what you pay for," does not apply here. You pay, all right, but you don't get. At least you don't get very much. The copywriter who thought up the name "Hungry Man Dinners" has seemingly never been, or ever fed, a truly hungry man.

So make your own frozen dinners! They are convenient, no doubt about it. And believe it or not, they can be delicious as well.

LEFTOVER DINNERS

These are dinners you can make for the family. Or, if you really don't mind serving guests from aluminum foil trays, you can even serve them to company with pride. Here's all you need to know.

- You can buy aluminum foil TV dinner trays at freezer supply stores, at many frozen-food locker plants, at some party goods stores, and at some discount stores or supermarkets. Buy a good supply.

166

- Remember this basic rule: *To freeze leftovers you must have moisture in which to heat the food, or it will stick and burn.* That's why commercial TV dinners feature meats with gravies, vegetables with juices or butter, or items such as fried chicken or french fries in which the oil in the coating does the job.

- Here's a second rule: *Cover the frozen food tightly to avoid freezer burn.* In the case of homemade TV dinners, this means pinching foil over the aluminum tray, just as the food producers do. Then place the tray in the freezer carefully so that the contents will not spill.

- When you cook a meal that would lend itself to making TV dinners, deliberately make extras. Here are some possibilities. Mix or match as you choose.

Meat	Vegetable	Starch
pot roast	carrots	mashed potatoes
burgers in gravy	string beans	french fries
creamed fish	spinach	potatoes au gratin
swiss steak	broccoli	corn
chicken à la king	swiss chard	buttered peas
pork patties	brussels sprouts	macaroni and cheese

Get the idea? Just remember to use a naturally moist food, or, as with the corn, use a little of the water in which it was cooked along with a pat of butter.

In making your own leftover TV dinners, you aren't limited to the traditional three-section tray, of course. You can freeze main-dish leftovers; and, by the time you make a salad and a dessert to complete your meal, you can have an entire dish thawed and heated.

Here are a few possibilities for leftover main dishes. These may be frozen in large aluminum pans and served family style, or, if you prefer, you can use smaller rectangular pans and give people their choice of individual entrées. With a salad, garlic bread, and dessert, all you need for a feast is leftover, frozen spaghetti with meat sauce or meatballs, beef stew, quiche Lorraine, lasagna, chicken paprika, pizza, beef stroganoff—use your imagination! Again, be sure the dish you plan to freeze and then heat has liquid in which it can cook and that it is sealed carefully.

The trick is to think ahead and to cook extra when you can. Then, when you're tired, rushed, or when the kids are cooking for themselves, all it takes to get dinner is to open the freezer and turn on the oven. Some working couples have found that it pays to cook lots of leftovers on weekends and to make several TV dinners. By planning a variety of weekend menus, they can quickly accumulate enough frozen dinners to allow for a real variety in the freezer. During the week, when they come home, the husband, for example, may select swiss steak, while his wife has creamed fish or whatever; and dinner can "cook" while they shower and relax before enjoying a really convenient, delicious meal!

COOK-AHEAD MEALS

It's hard to draw the line between deliberately cooked leftovers and cook-ahead dinners. But certain items lend themselves so well to freeze-ahead dinners that they deserve special mention.

Soup and Sandwich

Soups freeze great! It's well worth the trouble to make a big batch of soup just for freezing.

The same is true of sandwiches. You can make practically any type of sandwich, wrap it well in foil or plastic, freeze it, and when you're ready to eat it, let it thaw. To prepare the world's most convenient lunch, just take a container of frozen soup and frozen sandwiches out of the freezer at breakfast time. By lunchtime, the sandwiches will be thawed to room temperature and ready to eat. The soup will just require a little heating.

Here are a few tips:

- If you freeze soup in glass jars, don't fill them to the brim. Allow for expansion, or you'll have a real mess in the freezer. Use wide-mouth jars.

- Do label the soups. Frozen and frosty, it's hard to tell split pea soup from chicken gumbo.

- Do use butter, mustard, or catsup on your sandwiches. Do *not* use mayonnaise, because it will separate and make a mess. Do not garnish the sandwiches with lettuce, celery, or tomatoes, or they will become very soggy. You can use pickles or onions, but expect them to lose their crisp texture. Better to add garnishes as you serve the sandwiches.

Pizza

Frozen pizza is easy to make. Here's how.

Make:

a batch of Absolutely Easy Yogurt Bread (page 31)

Enough dough for 2 loaves will make several large pizzas. Exact measurements are impossible, because some people like thick crust, others thin; some like lots of sauce, some just a little.

Cut the dough into pieces. Generally, a ball of dough about 3 inches in diameter will make an average-sized pizza crust.

Coat the pizza pans with:

lecithin pan coating (page 214) OR *vegetable oil*

and roll out the dough in the pan. A small floured drinking glass makes a great rolling pin for this. Leave a turned-up, thick crust at the edge.

Cover the crust with:

1 cup marinara spaghetti sauce

Or use whatever sauce is your favorite.

Season the pizza with:

> garlic powder to taste   oregano to taste
> salt to taste

Cover the pizza with:

¼ pound thin-sliced mozzarella cheese

then dust with:

> grated Parmesan cheese

To freeze, place the pizza, right on the pan and *uncovered,* in the refrigerator until chilled. Then, still in the pan and still uncovered, place it carefully in the freezer so that it is level. It will freeze solid within a few hours. Then remove it from the pan if you wish, but in any case do wrap or cover it carefully with foil or plastic wrap.

To cook, unwrap the pizza and replace it, still frozen, on the pan if it was stored without one. Bake in a preheated 350-degree oven until the cheese is melted and browning and the crust is done— about 30 minutes.

You will need to buy several pizza pans to make your own frozen pizza in quantity; and since dough making is a bit of trouble, you might as well make a bunch. But the pans will pay for themselves the first or second time out. And you'll have additive-free pizzas sitting right in your freezer when friends or kids drop in!

Casseroles and Stews

When you make a casserole or stew, make two. Cook one for dinner. Freeze one for later. All it takes is aluminum foil and a casserole dish. Here's the easy way to do it.

Line a spare casserole dish with foil. Fill it with the casserole or stew mixture. Freeze the casserole completely. Slip the frozen casserole out of the dish. Wrap it completely with foil and store it in the freezer. To heat and serve, simply put the whole thing back into the dish in which it was molded, and bake. To save energy, allow it to thaw partially first.

WHAT NOT TO FREEZE

Freezing keeps food better and longer than any other method. It inhibits the development of the bacteria that cause spoilage. You can freeze most foods easily and safely. But don't try to freeze the following:

- Eggs. Raw eggs will crack. Hard-cooked eggs will get tough. You can freeze scrambled eggs, however. If you do, freeze the eggs in an ice cube tray, then store the cubes in a plastic bag. When someone wants quick scrambled eggs, thaw them right in a warm pan!
- Boiled potatoes. Yes, you can use them in TV dinners. But in soups, they will break up easily.
- Gelatin salads and desserts. They get goopy as they thaw.
- Mayonnaise or sour cream will separate.
- Creamy pies, desserts, and custards.

Do freeze whatever makes life easier and more convenient for you. And freeze items that will save you money and avoid additives. The main thing to remember about making frozen dinners is just that—to remember. If you make preparing extra a habit, you'll have convenience you never imagined possible—and save money to boot!

Chapter 20

Fun-to-Make-and-Eat Snacks

NEXT TIME you're at the supermarket, take a look at your shopping cart before you go through the checkout. Chances are you'll find some or all of these items: potato chips, pretzels, corn chips, flavored popcorn, salted nuts, fancy crackers, or any of the literally hundreds of snack items that cater to our urge to munch and crunch when we entertain, watch TV, read, or what have you. We are an oral society.

There are three major problems involving most of the snack items you might find in your grocery cart:

1. HIGH PRICE. Figure out the cost per pound of potato chips versus the cost per pound of potatoes. Or of bagged salted popcorn versus the do-it-yourself variety. Snacks are extremely expensive, and they account for a sizable percentage of the total grocery bill for many families.

2. LACK OF NUTRIENTS. How many vitamins are in a bag of cheese puffs? Or most of the other popular snacks? You already know the answer!

3. ADDITIVES. Many pretzel manufacturers achieve that nice shiny crust by dipping the pretzels into lye—yes, lye—before baking. In 1976 this resulted in an enormous recall when something went wrong and an excess amount of lye burned a few consumers' mouths. Some potato chips are preserved with BHA and BHT; many snacks are "flavor enhanced" with monosodium glutamate; and artificial colors and flavors abound. If you want a real shock, just read the label on a can of dip or spread. Then put it back on

the shelf. Don't worry. It won't rot. And some poor unsuspecting person will eventually buy it.

You and your family can munch healthfully, however. And less expensively. *When you make your own food.* The following make-your-own-food recipes are included in this chapter:

Appalachian Trail Ration

The Appalachian Trail runs from Maine to Georgia, and each year hundreds of hardy souls hike the length of it, becoming, in trail jargon, "end-to-enders." Thousands hike portions of the trail. And many of these hikers munch the following snack for energy as they trek along. People who only like to think about others hiking the trail eat it, too, because it's so delicious!

In a large bowl, mix:

1 cup raw almonds   *½ cup raw cashews*
1 cup raw pumpkin seeds   *½ cup raisins*
2 cups raw sunflower seeds *½ cup carob candy bits*
½ cup broken walnuts

Stir and eat. All of these seeds, raw, hulled, and ready to eat, are available at any good health food store. If you can find them in bulk, you'll save money. In any case, you'll find this is a snack that everyone will love and that even the youngest child can make. Store in a covered container in a dry place. *Makes 6 cups.*

VARIATIONS   Add or subtract any varieties of fresh raw nuts or seeds that you wish. Try it with chopped pitted dates or coarsely chopped dried apples. Delete the carob candy bits if you wish to reduce the sugar.

Dry-roasted Nuts

While you're at that health food store buying nuts in bulk, pick up a few pounds of raw, shelled peanuts.
In a large bowl, place:

1 *pound raw, shelled peanuts*   1 *teaspoon salt*
2 *tablespoons tamari sauce*

Stir until the nuts are thoroughly coated. Spread on two cookie sheets and bake in a preheated 250-degree oven until the nuts are done. This will take about 30 minutes. Stir frequently to avoid burning. To see if the nuts are done, allow a few to cool and taste them. Cool thoroughly before storing in a covered container in a dry place. *Makes 1 pound.*

These are the best dry-roasted nuts you've ever tasted. And they cost less than what you'll pay for nuts at the market.

VARIATIONS   Use any raw nut in place of the peanuts, or use a mixture of nuts.

For an unusual variation, sprinkle with 2 tablespoons sugar just before removing from the oven.

If you like your nuts slightly oily, add 2 tablespoons oil and 1 teaspoon liquid lecithin (this is vital!) to the tamari-salt mixture and whip it thoroughly with a spoon *before* adding the nuts. This will result in a thin, even coating of oil and tamari. Bake according to directions.

Potato Chips

Anyone can make homemade potato chips, but it's messy, so make a lot while you're at it. You can freeze any you don't plan to eat right away without losing their crispness.

Use a slicer or a very sharp knife to uniformly slice paper thin:

3–5 pounds scrubbed, unpeeled potatoes

Meanwhile, in a deep saucepan or electric deep fryer, heat:

4 cups vegetable oil

to *hot*—350 degrees if you have a thermometer or thermostat, or, if you don't, to the point that a drop of water will sizzle in the oil. The 4 cups of vegetable oil are necessary to provide enough depth to fry the chips evenly. Obviously, if you use a commercial deep fryer, you should follow the manufacturer's instructions on quantities of oil.

Deep fry the potato slices in small batches. Use a slotted spoon to remove them as soon as they are done, which will be when they are golden brown. Allow them to drain on a layer of paper towels covering a thick layer of newspapers. When all of the chips have been cooked, sprinkle them lightly but evenly with:

salt to taste

Makes 1 or 2 pounds of chips.

HINTS: You cannot make potato chips in a wok, because the shape prevents them from crisping evenly.

You can store uneaten chips for about a week in a closed container or for several months in a freezer. Put the chips to be frozen in a sealed plastic bag and be careful that other frozen foods don't crush them.

VARIATION   Try making potato chips from sweet potatoes for an unusual taste treat!

Corn Chips

Corn chips have an unusual characteristic. Like peanuts, once you start to eat them, you can't stop. Back in 1932, C. Elmer

Doolin, an out-of-work candymaker, discovered this when he had lunch in a small Mexican restaurant where corn chips were served as a garnish with his sandwich. He liked them so much that he bought the recipe from the cook for $100, which he raised from members of his family. He and his family then began cooking in their garage—and Fritos were born.

Here's how to make your own delicious corn chips at home.

In a blender or food processor, place:

2 eggs	1 cup unbleached white flour
2½ cups water	1 cup yellow cornmeal

Blend until well mixed. In a lightly greased frying pan, make extra-thin pancakes, cooking over medium heat until just done through but not brown. Do not turn. Dust with cornmeal, and stack the "pancakes" until all of the batter has been cooked.

Cut with a pizza cutter or sharp knife into traditional or fancy shapes. Carefully deep fry small batches of the strips in:

4 cups vegetable oil (350 degrees)

Follow the directions for deep frying as given in the recipe for Potato Chips (page 175). Drain on paper towels over a layer of newspapers. Sprinkle evenly with:

salt to taste

and allow to cool. Serve to hungry TV watchers with something tall, cold, and wet! *Makes about 1½ pounds of chips.*

VARIATIONS   Try adding any of the following to the basic mixture:

several drops of Tabasco sauce and 1 teaspoon paprika	1 tablespoon grated Parmesan cheese and ½ teaspoon oregano
1 teaspoon garlic powder and 1 teaspoon onion powder	
1 teaspoon celery seeds and 1 teaspoon caraway seeds	

The possibilities are endless!

Fantastic Dip

Dip homemade potato chips (see page 174) or corn chips (opposite) into one of these variations of a great dip.

To make the base, in a bowl, blender, or food processor, whip:

1 8-ounce package cream   ¼ cup milk
cheese, softened

Now stir in one of these combinations:

4 chopped cooked Better 'n   shrimp, drained, and ¼ tea-
Bacon strips (page 76) and   spoon thyme
2 tablespoons horseradish OR   1 teaspoon paprika, 3 shakes
½ finely chopped medium   of Tabasco sauce, ½ tea-
onion   spoon garlic powder, and
¾ cup chopped cooked shrimp   ½ teaspoon onion powder
OR 1 4½-ounce can cooked   ½ cup chopped pimientoes

Makes about 1½ cups of dip.

Again, use your imagination. Try to complement the other items on your menu.

Homemade Melba Toast

Check the price of packaged melba toast on your next trip to the market. Then make your own!

Use:

1 loaf of your favorite homemade bread

The texture of the bread should be almost cakelike as opposed to the soggy, spongy texture of store-bought white bread. Slice the bread *thin*—¼ inch is perfect. Cut the slices carefully into quarters. Spread the pieces on cookie sheets, not quite touching, and bake in a preheated 250-degree oven until lightly toasted on one side. Turn the slices over and repeat.

Now, here's the secret. Turn the oven down to the lowest setting and let the toasted bread pieces dry out completely for a few hours. The result will be the nicest homemade melba toast you can imagine. And a great homemade cracker substitute, too! *Makes about 1 pound of melba toast.*

Deviled Ham Spread

To make a tasty spread for your homemade melba toast (see page 177), grind in a blender or food processor:

  2 *cups leftover ham bits*

Empty into a bowl. Add:

  2 *tablespoons Extended*   ¼ *cup chopped onion*
    Butter, softened (page 211) ¼ *cup chopped pickles*
  1 *tablespoon mayonnaise*

Mix until you have a nice spreadable consistency. Add additional butter if needed. Store, covered, in the refrigerator. *Makes about 2¾ cups.*

NOTE: Unless you buy specially cured ham in a health food store, the ham will be cured with sodium nitrate and/or sodium nitrite, which are undesirable additives. However, because deviled ham is such a traditional spread, this recipe has been included. You can make an acceptable substitute by using Better 'n Bacon (page 76) instead of ham.

Peanut Butter

Did you know that the FDA allows commercial peanut butter to contain 50 insect fragments or 2 rodent hairs per 100 grams (that's 3½ ounces)? That doesn't mean it does contain it—but it can be so contaminated and still pass muster.

If you have a blender or food processor, you can make peanut butter without insect parts, rodent hairs, hydrogenated fats, BHA, BHT, or even salt if you wish. Here's how.

In a blender or food processor, grind:

1 pound roasted, unsalted peanuts

You can get them at your health food store. They will quickly turn to a coarse dust. Add:

1 teaspoon salt (or to taste)

Here's the trick that makes it work. Remove the blender lid or processor pusher and slowly, a drop or two at a time, right in the center of the whirling ground peanuts, add a bit of salad oil. Keep doing so until—whoosh—all of a sudden you have peanut butter! It will take altogether about:

1 tablespoon of vegetable oil

(An exact amount is impossible to give because the peanuts will vary in their natural oil content.) Scrape the peanut butter from the container, and if you want a larger quantity, repeat the process. Store in a covered jar in the refrigerator. *Makes 1 pint.*

VARIATIONS   Try one of the following:

Instead of peanuts, use roasted, salted cashew pieces, which are often sold at a lower price than whole cashews, omitting the salt from the recipe. Refrigerate for a day or two before eating so that the flavor can develop.

While the peanut butter is still warm and a bit runny, stir in:

½ cup honey

While the peanut butter is still warm, stir in:

½ cup toasted sesame seeds

Pretzel Rods

Why make homemade pretzels? Here are a few good reasons. As stated in the beginning of this chapter, some manufacturers coat their pretzels with lye to give them a shiny coating; you may wish to eat pretzels containing less salt than you would get in commercial pretzels; you may want to make interesting flavor variations for a party treat.

Start by making:

bread dough enough for 1 loaf

Food Processor Bread (page 32) is fine. After kneading, cut the dough into ¼-pound chunks. With a rolling pin, roll out each chunk of dough until it is ¼ inch thick. Using a pizza cutter, slice the rolled dough into ½-inch-by-8-inch strips. Place these strips on oiled cookie sheets, not touching, and brush them lightly with:

beaten egg

and dust with:

coarse salt to taste

Allow to rise in a warm place until they are about ¾ inch high. Then bake in a preheated 350-degree oven for about 15 minutes. Reduce the heat to 200 degrees and continue to bake for another 15 minutes, or until the pretzels are an even medium brown. If they are still slightly soft inside, reduce the heat to the lowest possible setting and allow them to dry out completely. *The equivalent of 1 loaf of bread dough yields about 3 dozen pretzel rods.*

VARIATIONS For a Philadelphia-type treat, don't allow the rods to dry out. Serve them soft, slightly warm, and spread with lots of yellow mustard.

Add 2 teaspoons of celery seeds to the bread dough.

Top with poppy seeds instead of salt.

Chapter 21

Beverages That Save You Money

HERE's a way to use the most popular cola drink: If your car battery terminals get really caked with the green gunk that causes poor connections and hard starts, just buy a bottle of cola, open it, and pour it slowly over each terminal. The corrosion will soften and wash away.

If you drink enough of it, so will your teeth.

Nutrition expert Dr. Clive McCay testified before a congressional committee that while he was doing nutritional research for the navy during World War II, he made the following discovery: "At the Naval Research Institute, we put human teeth in a cola beverage and found they softened and started to dissolve within a short period."

Why? Again from Dr. McCay, "The acidity of cola beverages . . . is about the same as vinegar. The sugar masks the acidity, and children little realize they are drinking this strange mixture of phosphoric acid, sugar, caffeine, coloring and flavoring matter."

Incidentally, until recently, about 80 percent of all the saccharin consumed has been used in diet soda pop.

From an economic standpoint, you pay just about the same price for soft drinks as for milk. Compare the prices. But, oh, the difference in nutritive values! Your quart of soda, in addition to dubious chemicals, 365 calories, and 93 grams of carbohydrates, contains no protein, no important minerals, no vitamins. On the other hand, a quart of milk contains 660 calories, 32 grams of protein, 48 grams of carbohydrates, and significant amounts of iron, calcium, phosphorus, and potassium as well as vitamins A, B complex, C, and D. Which is the better value?

Of course, you can't drink just milk. It would be both monotonous and fattening. But you can easily make delicious beverages at home with no real sacrifice in convenience and at a small fraction of the price you've been paying for beverages at the market.

Everyone wants to drink various beverages in addition to water. Beverages add interest to a meal. They help create a friendly atmosphere for entertaining. They offer a pleasant break in routine or a pick-me-up for the kids when they come home from school. Sometimes a nutritious beverage can even substitute for a meal.

Many commercial beverages are filled with sugar, which is nothing but empty calories, and chemicals that reputable scientists claim cause various diseases ranging from birth defects to hyperactivity in children to cancer. For example:

- All soft drinks contain acid and sugar. But you can make your own with little acid and they are delicious and lower in calories.
- Coffee contains caffeine, a dangerous, addictive drug. And decaffeinated coffee contains residues of trichloroethylene, a substance used to remove caffeine that the National Cancer Institute has reported causes cancer in laboratory animals. You can make your own coffee substitute at a fraction of the cost—and with real nutritive value.
- Instant breakfast mixes do give you a lift. But check the chemicals on the label—and the price. With some savings and with no sacrifice in convenience, you can make your own.
- Commercial wine may, by law, contain some seventy-seven chemical additives. Good wine costs two dollars a fifth and up. You can make delicious wine, with no chemicals, for as little as twenty-five cents a fifth.
- Chocolate and cocoa drinks contain theobromine, a chemical cousin to caffeine that is just as addictive and potentially dangerous. You can make delicious chocolatelike drinks without chocolate, with little or no sugar, and at very low cost.
- A popular canned punch advertises on TV, "Contains 10 percent real fruit juice!" Imagine that! And at 100-percent-fruit-

juice prices, too. Make your own with no additives, lots of nourishment, and for pennies a serving—with little more work than opening a can.

You can easily make a variety of beverages that you and your family will enjoy. Here are the recipes you'll find in this chapter:

COLD DRINKS

You are aware of the undesirable characteristics of commercial soft drinks. But have you taken a look at the labels on powdered drink mixes? Or on liquid concentrates? Have you checked the prices?

How much time does it really save you just to open a can as opposed to mixing a few items in your kitchen? A few minutes? Consider this. By taking a few minutes you can help your family avoid those undesirable additives. And you can save really big money. If making it yourself takes three minutes and saves you ten cents, that translates out to the equivalent of your earning two dollars an hour. And that's quite a saving in your food budget!

Some of the following recipes call for club soda. If you're not keen on carbonation, substitute plain water. And if you use a lot of club soda, consider buying a siphon bottle. With carbon dioxide cartridges, you can make sparkling water from tap water at one-third the commercial cost. And you can be sure that no sodium compounds have been added.

Low-Cal or Noncaloric Soda

For each serving, dissolve in a small amount of warm water in the bottom of a tall glass:

1 teaspoon sugar (or to taste)

Stir in:

12 dashes of Angostura bitters

Add ice. Slowly pour in approximately:

1 cup club soda

Stir gently and serve.

For a noncaloric drink, omit the sugar. If you like, garnish with a sprig of fresh mint or a slice of orange and serve with a straw.

Low-Cal Gingerale

For each serving, dissolve in a small amount of hot water in the bottom of a tall glass:

1 rounded teaspoon sugar   *⅛ teaspoon ground ginger*

Allow this to steep for several minutes so that the ginger flavor will come out. Add ice. Slowly pour in approximately:

1 *cup club soda*

Stir gently and serve.

Homemade Cream Soda

For each serving, dissolve in a small amount of warm water in the bottom of a tall glass:

1 *rounded teaspoon sugar*   ½ *teaspoon pure vanilla extract*

Add ice. Slowly pour in approximately:

1 *cup club soda*

Stir gently and serve.

Real Fruit Pop

For each serving, add to a tall glass filled with ice:

½ *cup any fruit juice*

Slowly pour in:

1 *cup club soda*

Stir gently and serve.

Keep in mind that fruit juices vary in intensity of flavor. For a strong-flavored juice, such as grape, decrease the amount of juice to ¼ cup. For a weaker-flavored juice, such as apple, increase the proportion to half juice, half club soda.

VARIATIONS Combine different flavors. Always use full-strength natural juices. Sugar can be added for those who have a real sweet tooth.

Dr. Jarvis's Tonic

This is a super pick-me-up, based on a recipe for old-time swizzle made famous by Dr. Jarvis, the Vermont physician who caused honey and cider vinegar to have a new surge in popularity.

For each serving, put into a tall glass:

2 teaspoons honey, prefer-   *2 teaspoons apple cider vinegar*
ably raw honey

Stir in enough water to dissolve. Add ice. Fill with water and stir.

On a hot day, this is a delightfully refreshing substitute for sugared iced tea. Old-time New England farmers carry a jug of this tonic on their tractors as they work in the fields.

VARIATION   For an effervescent version, substitute club soda for the water.

Natural Grape Punch

Combine and serve in a punch bowl over ice:

juice of 2 lemons   *2 cups grape juice*
juice of 4 oranges   *water to make 1 gallon*
½ cup honey dissolved in 1 cup
hot tea

Garnish with thin orange slices if desired. *Makes about 2 dozen 5-ounce servings.*

VARIATION   For an alcoholic punch, substitute a fifth of vodka or gin for an equal amount of water.

HOT DRINKS

Coffee prices are sky-high. Paying a manufacturer to mix cocoa powder, instant nonfat dry milk, and sugar into an expensive "convenience food" doesn't make sense when you can do it yourself.

However, there are good buys in hot drinks, with no caffeine or dangerous chemicals, right on the supermarket shelves. These are the various herb teas. If you've never tried some of the more delightful ones such as alfalfa-mint, chamomile, or rose hip, you don't know what you've been missing. Don't buy the expensive tea bags. Buy herb teas in bulk and use a tea ball. You'll save money.

NOTE: Most herb teas taste best sweetened with honey. However, blackstrap molasses makes a delicious sweetener for chamomile tea. Try it and see!

Or consider drinking the least expensive beverage of all—a cup of plain hot water, with or without a few drops of lemon juice. More and more people are doing just this and claim they find it quite satisfying.

"Chocolaty" Instant Carob Drink

Combine and store in an airtight container:

2 cups instant nonfat dry milk   ¼ cup sugar
¾ cup powdered carob

Makes 3 cups of mix; or 16 servings of hot drink or 24 servings of cold drink.

To make 1 serving of a hot drink

In a teacup, combine:

3 tablespoons of mix   boiling water to fill

Stir until dissolved.

Add:

¼ teaspoon pure vanilla extract for extra zip

To make 1 serving of an iced drink

In a blender, combine:

2 tablespoons of mix   *¼ teaspoon pure vanilla*
1 cup cold water   *extract*

Blend for a few seconds and serve over ice.

This makes a quick, nutritious, and inexpensive after-school drink for children.

VARIATION For fewer calories, omit the sugar.

Molasses Instant "Coffee"

In a teacup, combine:

1 tablespoon blackstrap   *hot water to fill*
molasses (or to taste)

Add:

milk OR *cream to taste*

Makes 1 serving.

VARIATION This tastes even better iced.

Sunflower Seed "Coffee"

Place in an ungreased shallow baking pan:

½ pound raw sunflower seeds

Roast in a preheated 350-degree oven for about 40 minutes, or until the seeds turn a uniform medium dark brown. Stir frequently to prevent burning. Do *not* overcook.

Next, grind the roasted seeds in a blender or food processor to the consistency of ground coffee. After this, if they have been roasted the proper amount, they should be the same color as ground coffee.

Store in an airtight container.

For each serving, boil together for 3 minutes:

1 coffee-measure ground seeds   *8 ounces water*

The grounds will absorb some of the liquid. Strain through a piece of coffee filter paper and serve. *Half a pound of sunflower seeds yields about 16 servings.*

This beverage tastes remarkably like coffee, yet costs far less and contains no harmful caffeine, no chemical residues from extracting caffeine, and no coffee oils.

Spiced Tea

You'll get frequent, if not constant comments about this delicious variation of plain old tea. And compare the price—commercial spiced tea costs over twice as much as plain tea.

Place in a tea ball:

1 tablespoon loose tea   *approximately 1 square-inch*
6 cloves   *orange peel, cut into small*
                                  pieces

Immerse the tea ball in:

3 cups boiling water

Steep as usual. *Makes 4 6-ounce servings*

VARIATIONS Use different teas. A rich Chinese type is delicious prepared this way. So is a hearty pekoe. Be creative!

Mocha

You can buy it ready-mixed, but it's expensive. Mocha is nothing but coffee mixed with chocolate. So to make a drink that will warm the coldest winter night . . .

In a teacup, combine:

1 cup steaming coffee to fill   *cream to taste*
1 healthy teaspoon chocolate
syrup

Makes 1 serving.

VARIATION   For a healthful variation, substitute a cup of Sunflower Seed "Coffee" (page 188) for the regular coffee and, for the other ingredients, 1 heaping teaspoon powdered carob, 1 heaping teaspoon instant nonfat dry milk, and whole milk to taste.

LIQUID BREAKFAST DRINKS

What is commercial instant breakfast? Read the label at the market. You're paying a huge premium for instant nonfat dry milk, sugar, flavoring—often artificial—and a lot of chemical vitamins and preservatives.

Make your own delicious, creamy liquid breakfast just as quickly with a blender, or even an egg beater or a spoon. If you want extra vitamins, take some pills. It's cheaper than paying a food manufacturer to add them for you.

Vanilla Liquid Breakfast (Basic Recipe)

Combine in a blender and whip until smooth and frothy:

½ cup instant nonfat dry milk   *1 teaspoon or more honey*
1 cup whole milk   *(optional)*
1 teaspoon pure vanilla extract

Serves 1.

This also makes a nourishing after-school snack for children. However, don't let them drink it too late in the afternoon, because it really "sticks to the ribs" and could spoil their dinner.

VARIATION For extra nutrition, substitute 1 cup plain yogurt for the cup of whole milk.

"Chocolate" Liquid Breakfast

Combine in a blender and whip until smooth and frothy:

½ *cup instant nonfat dry milk*
1 *cup whole milk*
1 *teaspoon pure vanilla extract*

1 *teaspoon or more honey*
  (optional)
2 *tablespoons powdered carob*

Serves 1.

Fruit-Flavored Liquid Breakfast

Combine in a blender and whip until smooth and frothy:

½ *cup instant nonfat dry milk*
1 *cup whole milk*
1 *teaspoon pure vanilla*
  extract

1 *teaspoon or more honey*
  (optional)
10 *medium strawberries* OR
  1 *medium banana*

Serves 1.

The banana liquid breakfast is especially nourishing and really fills you up!

Eggnog Liquid Breakfast

Combine in a blender and whip until smooth and frothy:

½ cup instant nonfat dry milk	1 teaspoon or more honey
1 cup whole milk	(optional)
1 teaspoon pure vanilla	1 egg
extract	¼ teaspoon nutmeg

Serves 1.

WINES

Wine is simply fermented fruit juice. And all the fermentation process consists of is feeding sugar to yeast. The yeast, in turn, makes carbon dioxide and alcohol as by-products. The carbon dioxide, a harmless gas, bubbles off. The alcohol remains in the juice, turning it into wine. When the concentration of alcohol reaches 14 percent, the yeast dies; and the wine is ready to clear and drink.

In October 1978, President Carter signed a bill that made it unnecessary to obtain a license to make wine in the home. Formerly, wine could be made in the home only by a "head of household" who had obtained a permit from the Treasury Department. Now, any single person over the age of 18 may legally make up to one hundred gallons of wine per year, tax-free. The limit is two hundred gallons in a household of two or more people over the age of 18.

Equipment

You will need some basic equipment, but don't let this put you off. You can pick it up at any wine-maker's supply firm. Check the Yellow Pages of your telephone book for one near you. Resist the temptation or the salesman's pitch to buy all of those chemicals and concentrates that are available. You don't need them. Here is all you will need to make your own easy, inexpensive wine:

- A few clean glass gallon jugs. Don't buy these. Save your own or get them from friends.
- An equal number of air locks. These let the carbon dioxide bubble off but keep out air, which might cause your wine to turn to vinegar.
- Several packets of wine yeast.
- A yard or so of nontoxic plastic tubing. Any good hardware store will have this. Get the ⅜-inch-diameter size.
- A large plastic funnel.
- A little patience.

Plain Grape Wine

Here's a wine you'll be proud to serve.

Pour into a clean gallon jug:

1 pound sugar   1 quart hot water

Shake to dissolve the sugar. Add:

1 cup strong tea   1 6-ounce can frozen
1 6-ounce can frozen grape   lemonade concentrate
  juice concentrate

Almost, but not quite, fill the jug with:

cool water

Add:

⅕ packet wine yeast

Shake to mix, then cap with a water-filled air lock.

Place in a warm, not hot, place for about 6 weeks, or until the bubbling stops. Your wine is finished. Now you must clear it. Here's how:

Using the plastic tube, siphon the wine into another clean jug.

Discard the sediment (dead yeast) in the bottom of the first jug.

Dissolve in 1 ounce hot water:

　1 *teaspoon unflavored gelatin*

Add this mixture to the wine and shake to mix.

Cover by pressing a small square of aluminum foil over the top of the jug. Do not cork! Fermentation may continue for a while and literally "blow your cork."

　Your wine will take from 3 days to a few weeks to clear. When it does, it is ready to serve. However, it will improve a great deal if you allow it to sit in a cool spot for a few months. You will get a bit more sediment, so siphon again as needed. *Makes 4 standard fifths of wine.*

Apple Wine

　This is a delightful white wine that tastes nothing like the commercial variety, which is merely an alcoholic soda pop.

Pour into a clean gallon jug:

　1 *pound sugar*　　　　　　　1 *quart hot water*

Shake to dissolve the sugar. Add:

　1 *6-ounce can frozen*　　　　1 *6-ounce can frozen apple*
　　lemonade concentrate　　　　*cider concentrate* OR 1
　　　　　　　　　　　　　　　quart natural unsweet-
　　　　　　　　　　　　　　　ened apple juice

Almost, but not quite, fill the jug with:

　cool water

Add:

⅓ *packet wine yeast*

Shake, cap with a water-filled air lock, and set in a warm spot for about 6 weeks, or until fermentation stops.

Clear according to the directions given for Plain Grape Wine (page 193). *Makes 4 standard fifths of wine.*

NOTE: Some apple juice is high in natural pectin and may always have a slight haze.

Dandelion Wine

Old-timers will tell you of dandelion wine that was so potent it cracked grandpa's glass eye. Usually it was made in a crock; and, with air getting to it, the result was probably vinegar. At any rate, homemade wine, dandelion or not, stops working at 14 percent alcohol. So forget all those broken glass eyes that littered our ancestors' kitchens!

Pick large, fresh dandelion blossoms. Do not include the stems. Gather them away from the road to avoid pollution from auto exhaust.

Combine:

2 *quarts fresh dandelion* *blossoms*	2 *quarts water*

and boil for 30 minutes.

Pour into a clean gallon jug:

1¼ *pounds sugar*

Using a funnel and strainer, pour the hot dandelion extract over the sugar. Shake to dissolve. Add:

1 *6-ounce can frozen lemonade concentrate*

Almost, but not quite, fill the jug with:

cool water

Add:

⅓ packet wine yeast

Shake to mix, cap with a water-filled air lock, and set in a warm spot for about 6 weeks, or until fermentation stops.

Clear according to the directions given for Plain Grape Wine (page 193). Dandelion wine will take a bit longer to clear, but it is absolutely delicious. *Makes 4 standard fifths of wine.*

VARIATION   Substitute 1 quart fresh, unsprayed rose petals for the dandelion blossoms. Save this unusual wine for extra-special occasions.

General Wine-Making Tips

- The preceding recipes are for dry wine. If it's too dry for your taste, add a tiny bit of sugar when you serve it. Then, in subsequent batches, add a bit more sugar to the recipe—but no more than ¼ pound, or your wine will be too sweet.
- Yeast likes acid, hence the lemonade. You can use the juice of 2 fresh lemons instead, but add about an extra ¼ pound sugar if you do.
- The tea (see page 193) is for red wines. Tannin helps the wine to work.
- The gelatin for clearing is a step you can skip if you're in no hurry. It simply makes the dead yeast settle out faster.
- Experiment! Substitute cranberry juice for grape juice or pineapple juice for apple. Or use a mixture of juices. You'll always get good results with these simple, easy-to-follow directions.

WATER

Pure Water for Drinking and Cooking

It is a sad fact that much of the water supply in our society is contaminated to one degree or another. Samuel Epstein, M.D., professor of occupational and environmental medicine at the University of Illinois Medical Center, has this to say in a letter:

"Most water in major municipalities is contaminated by a very wide range of organic pollutants which are not removed by conventional treatment at municipal filtration plants. Each homeowner can massively reduce the level of these contaminants by using reverse osmosis filtration units, or activated charcoal filtration units, which can be directly attached to the tap. For the latter, choose a unit in which the charcoal is impregnated with germicides, such as silver salts, to discourage bacterial and algal growth."

An inexpensive tap-type filter sells for under five dollars at many health food stores or through health food mail-order outlets. According to the manufacturers' ads, these last for some months. More elaborate filtration or distillation units are advertised frequently through such publications as *Prevention* magazine.

The point is, if you're serious about making a big reduction in harmful chemicals and substances in the food your family eats, you should consider making the same effort when it comes to the water they drink.

Chapter 22

Have Your Own Fast-Food Chain,
at Home

You've SEEN and probably visited the hamburger shops with the famous golden arches. And the sign out front that proclaims, "Over X-many Billion Sold." And does McDonald's sell 'em! Recent figures showed that one firm in upstate New York produced 45 percent of the hamburger patties for McDonald's, grinding up to 450 cattle a day to make burgers by the million.

It was also recently reported that the standard fast-food hamburger is 4¾ inches in diameter, which cooking reduces to exactly 4 inches. It weighs one-tenth of a pound, the same as a hot dog, and has 65 percent moisture, 17 percent protein, and 18 percent fat. But, of course, the big drawing card is the fancy burger with the "secret sauce." All in all, they're pretty good. But you can make them cheaper at home. And the kids won't be tempted to drink green milk shakes or sugary soft drinks either.

Like all food manufacturers, the fast-food chains rely on a few basic sales ideas. They've convinced people that they

- can make it taste better
- can make it cheaper
- can offer ultimate convenience
- have some special magic

Here's a list of the recipes in this chapter:

The Big Burger

Do your kids ever have a "big burger attack"? They will if you treat them to this!

Make your patties by mixing ground beef in the proportions of:

1 tablespoon tamari sauce to 1 pound lean ground beef

Shape into 4-ounce squares by pressing in a folded waxed paper envelope, or, if you're a purist and insist on round burgers, use a small burger press. Make a large supply; freeze them, not touching, on a cookie sheet; then store in a plastic bag.

To cook, use a hot griddle or frying pan and don't overcook. Top each with:

1 slice cheese

just before serving. Place on your own homemade sesame-seed-topped bun (see recipe on page 44) with a slice of tomato, a thin slice of onion, pickle chips, a bit of lettuce, and your own super, secret sauce.

Super, Secret Sauce:

Don't tell, but do mix together:

*2 parts homemade mayonnaise
  (see page 135)*

*1 part prepared mustard
1 part catsup*

Top your Big Burger with this and wait for the plaudits!

Super Sandwiches

There is only one original super sandwich. And anyone from Philadelphia will forget all about brotherly love to argue that it's a Philadelphia Hoagie. And a Bostonian will rise up with the claim that it's a Boston Grinder. And from other parts of the country will come shouts of "Submarine Sandwich!" "Hero Sandwich!" "Poor Boy!"

The fact is that all attest to the ingenuity of what a clever cook can do with a large loaf of French or Italian bread.

Philadelphia Hoagie:

Cut a loaf of Italian-style bread lengthwise, spread it open, and top with layers, in order, of:

capicola (sliced Italian hot *hot* OR *sweet pepper slices*
   ham) *salt*
salami *pepper*
provolone cheese *a pinch of oregano*
tomato slices *lettuce*

Fold together, cut into portions, and serve.

Boston Grinder:

Use the same ingredients as are in the hoagie but end up with the cheese. Allow the loaf to stay spread open, and broil for a few minutes until the cheese is melted and browned a bit.

NOTE: Unfortunately, most commercial luncheon meats contain sodium nitrate and/or sodium nitrite. You can get additive-free cold cuts at some health food stores; and, if you're lucky enough to have one nearby, some local meat processors still make pork products without dubious additives. These recipes are for those people who will either go to the trouble to find chemical-free luncheon meats or for those who will occasionally eat "store-bought" processed meats anyway.

VARIATIONS   Use any long loaf of bread, preferably homemade. Cut it open lengthwise and stuff with any combination of meats, cheeses, and condiments that appeal. Suggestions: Baked ham, cheese, tomato, lettuce, and Russian dressing. Thin roast beef piled high, topped with mustard and horseradish. Tuna salad topped with tomato slices and lettuce

---

Tomato Pie House Pizza

Pizza, as every "expert" on the subject will tell you, is simply the Italian word for pie, so calling it pizza pie is redundant. But as anyone who speaks Italian can tell you, *torta* is the Italian word for pie; and *pizza* isn't a regular Italian word any more than *hoagie* is, though those same "experts" will insist that these large sandwiches bear a solid Italian name. Actually, *pizza* may come from the old Italian word for *point,* since the succulent pies are traditionally cut into pieces that come to points.

To make yours, simply bake one of those frozen pizzas you made according to the recipe on page 169.

For a pizzeria touch, top with one or more of the following in addition to the cheese:

thin-sliced onions
thin-sliced green peppers
slices of cooked Italian
   sausage
pepperoni slices

anchovies
crumbled cooked ground
   beef
mushroom slices

Serve with chilled homemade red wine (see page 193).

Massachusetts Oven-Fried Chicken

You don't have to be a colonel to make this great chicken. Nor do you have to have the mess and extra calories of deep frying in order to get batter-dipped chicken.

Place in a blender or food processor:

1 *cup Pancake Mix* (page 53)
1 *egg*
⅓ *cup water*
1 *tablespoon vegetable oil*
1 *teaspoon tamari sauce*
½ *teaspoon salt*
⅛ *teaspoon ground black pepper*
¼ *teaspoon garlic powder*
¼ *teaspoon paprika*
¼ *teaspoon basil*

Whip and pour into a bowl. With this mixture, coat thoroughly:

1 *3-pound chicken, cut in pieces*

Spread the pieces, not touching, on a baking sheet and bake in a preheated 350-degree oven for 50 minutes, or until done. To test for doneness, cut into the thickest part of the meat to the bone and make sure that no pink shows. *Serves 4.*

Now, here's the gravy with the secret spices and herbs:

In a frying pan, heat:

2 *tablespoons vegetable oil*

Slowly add:

3 *tablespoons flour*

and stir until brown.

Add:

water

a little at a time, until you have a paste. Then add, a little at a time:

½ *can condensed chicken broth, undiluted (Sorry, they all seem to contain at least some MSG!)*

Continue to simmer as you add:

a dash of pepper	¼ teaspoon onion powder
a pinch of sage	¼ teaspoon sugar
a large pinch of thyme	2 teaspoons oyster sauce, if
a large pinch of basil	available (or substitute an
½ teaspoon paprika	equal amount of tamari
¼ teaspoon garlic powder	sauce)

If your gravy is too thick, add a little more water until it's just right for you.

Serve the chicken and gravy with mashed potatoes and cole slaw, and be sure to allow your family to lick their fingers!

Tacos

Start with tortillas. In a blender or food processor, mix:

2 eggs	1 cup yellow cornmeal
2½ cups water	½ teaspoon salt
1 cup unbleached white flour	

On a lightly greased griddle, make 4- to 5-inch pancakes, frying over medium heat for about 2 minutes, or until just barely done. Do not turn. As they become finished, stack, dusting between the layers with cornmeal.

Holding the tortilla in the classic taco "U" shape so that it can later be filled, lower it with tongs into:

4 cups vegetable oil (350 degrees)

If you use a commercial deep fryer, use the amount of oil recommended by the manufacturer. If you don't have a thermometer or an electric deep fryer with a thermostat, heat the oil until a drop of water sizzles in the oil. Frying will take about 2 minutes for the soft variety of tacos and about 5 minutes for the firm, crisp variety. Makes 18 tacos.

Fillings

Along with your tacos, offer a variety of filling ingredients, in separate bowls, that people can serve themselves. For example:

browned ground beef sea-   *coarsely shredded cheese*
soned with chili powder,   *taco sauce (Buy a can; as*
cumin, and garlic   *with prepared mustard*
shredded lettuce   *and catsup, it just isn't*
chopped onions   *worth making your*
diced tomatoes   *own!)*

French Fries

Every hamburger chain features french-fried potatoes. You'll find a good recipe for nonmessy, easy-to-fix oven french fries on page 110. Or, if you prefer to make the deep-fried variety, here's how.

For each person, scrub:

1 large potato

Don't bother to peel. Cut the potatoes into french-fry-size strips; remember that cooking will cause some shrinkage, so don't slice them *too* thin, unless you want shoestring potatoes.

In a deep saucepan or french fryer, heat:

4 cups vegetable oil OR *the amount specified for your french fryer*

The oil should be hot, about 350 degrees. Fry a small amount of potato strips at a time until just light brown. Drain on several thicknesses of paper towels, then set aside.

When all of the potato strips have been browned, and just before serving, fry the strips again until they are crisp and brown. This double-frying makes them crisper. Drain again and sprinkle with:

salt to taste

Serve immediately. Some people like french fries seasoned with catsup, others like them sprinkled with a few drops of vinegar, and others prefer them plain.

The Salad Bar

This is a recent innovation in some fast-food restaurants. But, of course, you can do it better. All you need is a table, a large serving bowl, and several smaller serving bowls. Let people help themselves.

In the large bowl, put:

washed and shredded lettuce

In the smaller bowls, put any of the following:

- sliced tomatoes
- sliced onions
- sliced cucumbers
- green pepper rings
- carrot sticks
- celery sticks
- strips of cheese
- pickle chips
- olives
- cold cooked shrimp
- flaked tuna fish
- cocktail sauce for the shrimp
- salad dressings

These are only suggestions, of course. Vary your salad bar according to the basic menu for the meal, your budget, and whatever you have available in the refrigerator or on the shelves.

Milk Shakes

Most fast-food restaurants offer a variety of soft drinks and milk shakes. Make your own by referring to the recipes in chapter 21, "Beverages That Save You Money." You'll find directions for making soda pop in the cold drinks section, and any of the liquid breakfast drinks would make fine "milk shakes" to go with your own fast-food-style meals. Or, if you prefer to serve old-fashioned ice cream milk shakes, they can easily be made at home.

In a blender, put:

1 *cup milk*	½ *teaspoon pure vanilla*
2 *scoops vanilla ice cream*	*extract*

Whip until light and frothy. *Serves 1.*

VARIATIONS For a "chocolate" milk shake, add 2 tablespoons carob powder. For strawberry, substitute strawberry ice cream for the vanilla ice cream.

Chapter 23

Make All Those Expensive Extras—Inexpensively

THINK back to before you began to make your own food. How many items in your shopping cart added up to lots of dollars for little in nutritive value? And with what chemicals were some of those items preserved, enhanced, colored, flavored, adulterated, and embalmed?

The fact is, you don't have to be a gourmet cook to make your own "extras" that can add excitement to your entertaining and family meals. Here are recipes for some assorted goodies that will make your cooking easier, earn you rave reviews, and let you bank the dollars you don't spend at the store. They include:

Seasoned Salt

Jane, Joan, Mary, or Bill, you have to be "crazy" if you don't make your own mixed-up salt! It's so easy! Here's how.

In a thoroughly dry blender, grind to the desired fineness:

½ cup coarse salt (rock-type sea salt is the best)

¼ cup granular kelp (inexpensive at any health food store)

1 teaspoon garlic powder

1 tablespoon basil

1 teaspoon peppercorns

Yields about 1 cup.

VARIATIONS You can make interesting variations on this delicious general seasoning. Here's one:

½ cup coarse salt

¼ cup granular kelp

1 teaspoon garlic powder

½ cup dried vegetable flakes

Yields about 1¼ cups.

Or this Italian-style seasoning:

½ cup coarse salt

¼ cup granular kelp

1 teaspoon garlic powder

1 teaspoon onion powder

1 tablespoon oregano

Yields about 1 cup.

Or this barbecue salt, which is delicious sprinkled on popcorn or homemade potato chips. Stir together:

½ cup regular salt (not extra fine)

1 teaspoon garlic powder

1 teaspoon onion powder

1 tablespoon paprika

½ teaspoon cayenne

Yields about ⅔ cup.

Try your own variations—tarragon for a French accent, ginger for Chinese, and so on. Experiment!

Bread Crumbs

Commercial bread crumbs are extremely expensive. The next time you're in the supermarket, check the price of 16 ounces of bread crumbs, the equivalent of 1 loaf of bread. Making your own bread crumbs takes only a few minutes and is a great way to use up any stale bread you may happen to have. Here's what to do.

On cookie sheets, place:

torn slices of any kind of bread

and put them in the oven at the lowest setting for a few hours, or until they are thoroughly dried out. Crumble the bread into a blender or food processor and grind it into crumbs. If you wish, mix in quantities, to taste, of:

salt	*garlic powder*
dried herbs	*grated Parmesan cheese*

Put the crumbs in a jar, preferably one with a shaker top, and use as needed. *Each slice of bread yields about ⅓ cup dry crumbs.*

That's all there is to it. And these crumbs made from home-made bread are delicious as well as cheap!

Sauce Mix

In a bowl, mix:

3 *tablespoons instant chicken soup mix (buy the Wyler brand at your supermarket or the various brands without MSG sold at health food stores)*

2¼ *cups instant nonfat dry milk*

1½ *cups unbleached white flour*

2 *tablespoons dried parsley flakes*

1 *teaspoon garlic powder*

That's it! Store in an airtight container. And when you need a white sauce, simply melt:

2 *tablespoons Extended Butter* (page 211)

in a pan and stir in:

½ *cup mix*

Stirring constantly, add:

hot water

until the desired consistency is reached. Season with:

salt to taste

Makes about 4 cups mix, or enough to make sauce 8 times.

VARIATIONS Add Cheddar cheese for a sauce for cauliflower or other vegetables, or a few shakes of Tabasco sauce for piquancy. For a brown sauce, substitute 1 tablespoon tamari sauce for part of the water and omit the salt.

Quick Mushroom Gravy

Here's a fast gravy that goes with many dishes.

In a frying pan, heat:

2 cups sliced fresh mushrooms   *1 tablespoon Extended Butter* (opposite)

Cook over medium heat for several minutes, or until the mushrooms are done through. Add:

½ cup boiling water   *ground black pepper to*
2 teaspoons tamari sauce   *taste*

To thicken, shake together:

½ cup water   *2 tablespoons flour*

Slowly pour the flour and water into the simmering mushroom mixture, stirring constantly over moderate heat for a couple of minutes, or until thickened. *Makes 1½ cups.*

Extended Butter

How would you like a spread that tastes like butter, looks like butter, spreads soft, contains no chemical additives, is high in polyunsaturated fats, contains less salt, and costs one-third less than butter? A few minutes and a blender or food processor are all it takes. But you must follow these steps exactly and in order:

Put in a blender:

1 *cup vegetable oil (use a good unsaturated one such as safflower or corn oil)*

Add:

1 *teaspoon liquid lecithin*   5 *ounces (¼ cup plus 1 tablespoon) water*

Blend thoroughly. Then add:

1 *pound room-temperature butter*

Blend again, scraping down the sides of the container as needed. Scrape into a serving bowl and refrigerate. *Makes about 1¾ pounds.*

That's all there is to it! The water adds no calories but makes the mixture have a nice spreading consistency.

Here's how the extended butter stacks up against regular butter or margarine:

	Butter or Margarine	Extended Butter
Calories:	200 per ounce	180 per ounce
Fat:*	11% polyunsaturated	38% polyunsaturated
	89% saturated	62% saturated

* Fat content may vary widely in various types of margarine. A common brand was used here.

Food Processor Technique

Place the steel blade in the food processor. Then cut the butter into chunks and distribute them evenly around the food processor container. Secure the lid in place, turn on the processor, then slowly pour the remaining ingredients down the chute in this order: vegetable oil, liquid lecithin, water. Process until smooth and fluffy.

HINT: After you make the Extended Butter, don't just wash out the blender or food processor container right away. Use what sticks to prepare vegetables. Simply add 1 cup hot tap water to the container, swish it around to melt the butter, then pour it into a bowl and store it in the refrigerator until needed. Cook vegetables in this buttery water.

VARIATIONS Use salt-free butter instead of regular butter. If you like a bright yellow butter, whip in the juice from 1 carrot oil capsule. This also adds a lot of vitamin A.

Sweet Pickles

If you love pickles but hate the preservatives and colorings in so many commercial brands, try these. Unlike many other recipes, they are very easy and quick to make.

Bring to a boil:

  1 *cup water*   1 *cup sugar*
  1 *cup apple cider vinegar*   1 *teaspoon mace*

Add and let simmer for 6 minutes:

  about 3 large cucumbers, sliced

If you can't get the slices in the saucepan all at once, cook a portion, take them out with a slotted spoon, then cook the rest. Pack into a jar or jars, top with the juice from the saucepan, and chill. You may can these if you wish or simply prepare them as needed in batches this size. *Makes about 1 quart.*

VARIATION   During the cooking, add 1 small onion, sliced and separated into rings, ½ teaspoon garlic powder, and 1 teaspoon mustard seeds for bread-and-butter-style pickles.

Half-Sour Pickles

This is the greatest way in the world to use those summertime pickling cukes.

Get a large crock, cookie jar, or wide-mouth jug. Wash a quantity of:

pickling cucumbers

and cut just a bit from each end. Pack them, one at a time, in the crock, getting in as many as possible. Add:

water

pouring it into the crock just to the top of the cukes. Now pour this water into a separate container; you will use it as the base for your pickles, and what you have done is to measure the exact amount you will need.

Add the water to a cooking utensil, one cup at a time, keeping track of how many cups you have. For *each cup of water used*, add:

1 *teaspoon garlic powder*	2½ *tablespoons apple cider*
2 *teaspoons salt*	*vinegar*

Bring the mixture to a boil, then simply pour it over the cukes, which are still in the crock. Cover loosely and allow to sit at room temperature for 3 days. Then store in the refrigerator and enjoy.

Do NOT slice or otherwise cut the cucumbers, except for the small piece taken from each end, or they will get very mushy. This recipe is not recommended for any but pickling cucumbers.

Lecithin Pan Coating

You can buy a vegetable pan spray under various trade names. PAM is probably the best known. And if you've ever tried it, you know it works. Why? Because the active ingredient is liquid lecithin, a natural soybean-oil derivative that not only acts as an excellent emulsifier but also has the amazing property of making pans just about stick-free.

You can buy a spray can of lecithin diluted with something or other. Or you can save money and make your own in seconds. Here's how.

In a small jar, place:

1 cup vodka   *4 teaspoons liquid lecithin*

Shake. *Makes 1 cup.*

You now have a pan coating the equal of any on the market. Why not use the plain liquid lecithin? You can, but it is thick and messy and you would waste a lot. Why vodka? Well, why not? It dissolves the lecithin and makes it workable. And, as the pan heats, the vodka evaporates, leaving only the thin coating of lecithin. You're ready to cook on a stick-free but easy-to-wash surface. If the idea of vodka really bothers you, use corn oil instead. It works almost as well.

You can either brush on your pan coating or get a small spray bottle and spritz it on. However, the latter can get messy. Sometimes you can buy a small pan oiler with a dip-in cotton swab in a variety store. But a small piece of paper towel works just fine.

Chapter 24

Pet Foods Your Dog or Cat Will Love

READ any good dog food labels recently? If you have, you've probably noticed that Fido eats better than you do. Fact: Most—not all, but most—dog foods are better balanced nutritionally than the processed foods that people get. And they contain fewer chemicals.

The new "moist" dog foods, it's true, are filled with red dye to make them look appealing to you—Rover couldn't care less because he's color-blind anyway—and, as you may know, the law requires that ingredients be listed in order of their percentage of the contents of all foods, and this applies to dog food too. So just consider the ingredients in your favorite moist dog food, and you'll discover why Spot loves it. Or at least, eats it. It is loaded with sugar. Nice, fattening sugar.

A leading canned dog food doesn't list any artificial color or sugar, but does list water as the number-two ingredient. Water is harmless, but thirty-eight cents a pound is a bit steep to pay for it.

Here's the straight dope on pet foods. The dry kibbles from reputable companies are completely balanced, although you might want to add a bit of meat to up the amino acids that make a pet's urine acidic and thus help ensure against the formation of bladder stones. But let's face it. Would you eat kibble? Sure, if you're a farm dog tied up in the barn. But little Fifi begging for steak scraps is supposed to gag down that stuff while watching you gorge? Where's your heart, anyway?

Thus, many owners go the wrong route. They feed all-meat

products to dogs and cats and end up with pets suffering from severe dietary deficiencies, especially weakened bones from a lack of calcium. Or they let their cats ignore the unappetizing dry stuff and go hunt for small critters that are probably loaded with worms, which, in turn, infest the cats.

If you're really serious about this make-your-own-foods business, here are pet-food recipes that your household livestock will love— maybe, pets being the spoiled beasts that they are. They include:

Breakfast in a Saucer

A small saucer of milk is a fine breakfast. But here's a better one.

In a blender, put:

½ cup water
2 tablespoons instant nonfat
dry milk

1 teaspoon cod liver oil
½ teaspoon wheat germ oil

Blend and feed like plain milk. Great for either dogs or cats! *Makes enough to serve 1 cat or 1 20-pound dog.*

NOTE: Some dogs have difficulty digesting milk, and this recipe may cause diarrhea. If this problem applies to your pet, a small amount of Dog and Cat Cake (below) may be substituted to make up his or her daily calorie requirement.

Dog and Cat Cake

Dogs and cats should *not* eat an all-meat diet. They need minerals and vitamins that do not occur naturally in meat. This "cake" tastes good enough for you to enjoy; and, when mixed with meat and a small amount of broth, it makes a completely nutritious meal.

In a blender, put:

3 *cups water*
½ *cup corn oil*
2 *eggs*
2 *tablespoons cod liver oil*
1 *100-IU capsule vitamin E*
1 *low-potency multimineral
  capsule from your health*

*food store containing at
least copper, zinc, iron,
manganese, and magnes-
ium (Break open the pill
and add just the powder,
discarding the empty gel-
atin capsule.)*

Blend until the ingredients are thoroughly mixed. In a bowl, put:

2 *cups whole wheat flour*
1 *cup cornmeal*
¾ *cup instant nonfat dry milk*
½ *cup bran*
¼ *cup bone meal (vital—
  don't skip this!)*

¼ *cup brewer's yeast
  powder*
2 *tablespoons granular kelp*
1 *tablespoon double-acting
  baking powder*

After mixing the dry ingredients together, pour in the blended liquid ingredients all at once. Mix together thoroughly, pour into two greased layer-cake pans, and bake. This is important: Bake in a preheated 400-degree oven—this changes the starch into *dextrin*, which not only tastes good to your pet but makes it more digestible. When done, after about 25 minutes, cool on a rack as with any cake.

Directions for feeding follow.

Feeding Fido

The basic nutritional requirement for any animal is calories. If the critter doesn't eat, he'll starve. Each layer of Dog and Cat Cake contains about 1,200 calories. And, like people, dogs need the basic amino acids found in protein foods. So, for a twenty-pound pooch, cut one of the layers into 6 parts. Each part is 1 serving, providing 200 calories. To make a completely nutritious and sufficient meal, crumble and mix it with any one of the following combinations:

· 3 or 4 ounces ground beef cooked in a little water
· 2 scrambled eggs
· 4 ounces liver, chopped up and cooked with a little water

Get the idea? Or save money by giving Fido the healthful stuff you won't eat. Mix about 3 ounces of meat scraps with his dog cake. Or when you're pressed for time, mix in half a small can of all-meat dog food instead.

IMPORTANT: This feeding concept assumes that you are giving your pet the breakfast drink or a small amount of milk or whatever in the morning, because a twenty-pound dog needs about 750 calories a day; and the dog cake plus the meat provides only about 500 calories. Adjust the amount to the dog's weight, so that a forty-pound dog gets twice as much and so on.

Where is the convenience? Simple. It takes only minutes to make a twelve-day supply of dog food for an average small dog. And you can save money by having a built-in way to feed him those meat scraps in the most nutritious way. Store unused cake, wrapped, in the refrigerator. If you wish, bring to room temperature before serving.

VARIATION If you want an all-in-one food, cook 2¼ pounds of ground meat, combine it with the cake ingredients, and bake in four layer-cake pans. Just crumble and serve twice the quantity of plain Dog and Cat Cake.

Feeding Kitty

Those TV cats are finicky. But even if your cat isn't, keep these things in mind:

- Cats need more of certain vitamins than dogs do.
- Cats need more protein proportionately than dogs do. So make the basic Dog and Cat Cake, but double the cod liver oil and the brewer's yeast powder.

To make an all-in-one meal, follow the directions outlined above, substituting your cat's favorites, such as ground liver. By baking it right into the cake, you will have a semidry convenience food the cat can nibble on all day, which is the way many cats prefer to feed.

Or if you prefer, start with a one-sixth part of a layer of the basic cake mixed with half a can of cat tuna or 3 to 4 ounces of meaty table scraps or other meat food. The calories and so on work out just about the same as for dogs.

Amounts eaten vary widely from cat to cat, but you can quickly find the right amount to set out each day for yours.

Chapter 25

A Kitchen Drawer of

Professional Tips

THE RECIPES in this book have shown you how to make your own food. You are, after all, just as smart as Betty Crocker; and, while you may not command the army of chemists and technicians that General Foods does, you can win the war against high prices and chemicals while assuring yourself and your family of convenient, healthful, delicious, and nutritious foods.

Everyone has a drawer in his or her kitchen that is reserved for things that don't fit anywhere else. This chapter is a "kitchen drawer" full of professional odds and ends—tips that can help make your cooking even easier. They aren't recipes and they don't really fit into any standard cookbook chapter. But, then, this isn't exactly a standard cookbook.

These are the secrets of the pros. Read them and remember to use them when the occasion arises. They appear under these categories:

FOOD PREPARATION

- To cook pasta products more quickly, add a little vegetable oil to the water. This will prevent it from boiling over and will allow you to cover the pot and thus hasten the cooking time.

- If your oven scorches cookies on the bottom, use your cookie pan turned upside down. The pocket formed will tend to prevent burning.

- Where a recipe calls for separated eggs and you get a bit of yolk in with the whites, you can easily fish it out with the tip of a piece of cloth dampened with water. And, of course, remember to break eggs, one by one, into a small bowl first.

- If eggs crack while hard-cooking, sprinkle them generously with salt, which will seal the cracks.

- Actually, eggs should not crack during hard-cooking if they are first dampened with cold water before being put into boiling water.

- Best of all, start eggs in cold water and hard-cook at just below boiling for 20 minutes. Thus prevents cracking, ensures a pretty yellow yolk, and prevents rubbery whites.

- An old trick is to add 1 tablespoon of salt to each pint of water in which eggs will be hard-cooked. This is supposed to make them much easier to peel.

- When using potatoes as an extender, as in fish cakes, croquettes, or whatever, mashed baked potatoes instead of boiled give your fish a fluffier and lighter texture.

- A scant teaspoon of double-acting baking powder thoroughly mixed into poultry stuffing will help keep it light and avoid sogginess.

- When baking with nuts, raisins, dried fruits, and such, heat them in the oven briefly before adding them to the batter. This will keep them from sinking to the bottom of the baked goods.

- If you make your own whipped cream, and you should, and it whips a bit too long, add a little cold milk and whip again. You can restore it to a perfect texture.

- For that party salad, wash and dry your lettuce leaves, then dip the edges into a bowl of water that has a bit of paprika floating on top. It will fringe the leaves with red.

- To thicken gravy, always add flour to the water and not the other way around. Use a plastic jar with a tight-fitting lid; put in the water, add the flour, and shake.

- Never salt meat before or during cooking because it makes it tough and causes loss of moisture.

- To avoid soggy piecrusts, the bane of quiche lovers, brush the crust lightly with raw egg, bake for 10 minutes, then add the pie filling and bake as usual.

- To thin-slice raw meat, have it slightly frozen for easier handling.

- Here's a fast, festive hors d'oeuvre: Just stick thin pretzel sticks into small squares of cheese and serve. Edible toothpicks!

- There's nothing worse than soggy, leftover tossed salad, right? So . . . toss it in the blender, add tomato juice as needed, whip, chill, and presto—Gazpacho!

- Make whatever fruit is in season a festive dessert by cutting it up and soaking it in sweet homemade wine before serving.

- When you make whipped cream, make double the amount needed. Then spoon the extra into separate little piles on a cookie sheet and pop it into the freezer, uncovered. Freeze solid, then *quickly* pry loose and store in a plastic bag. You have instant individual toppings at your convenience.

- Make candy on a cool, dry day. Sticky weather can make sticky candy.

- Stale rolls? If you don't need bread crumbs, just sprinkle the rolls with water, place in a paper bag, and warm in a preheated 250-degree oven for 5 to 10 minutes. This will restore their freshness.

- To decorate salads, fill hard-cooked eggs, decorate cakes, or whatever, just put the filling (mayonnaise, egg mix, icing) into a small plastic bag, twist and seal, then snip off a corner. Just squeeze out the filling. You have an instant, disposable decorator.

- For punch, freeze ice cubes of fruit juices or the punch mix, and melting ice won't dilute your drink.

- Make square hamburger patties in advance by pressing them in folded squares of waxed paper. Then don't unwrap these squares, just pop them into a plastic bag and freeze. This way, you'll always have the fixin's for a fresh hamburger on hand. Just take out as many patties as you need from the bag, unwrap, and cook.

- To grease a pan and not your fingers, stick your hand inside a plastic bag. You've got a disposable glove.

- If you're going to use spices that don't get eaten, such as whole cloves, bay leaves, or garlic buds, put them in a tea ball before adding to the recipe. You'll save a fishing trip.

- To measure ½ cup of butter, fill a measuring cup half full with water. Add butter until the water reaches the 1-cup level. Then pour out the water. Use this method to measure any amount of solid shortening.

MONEY-SAVERS

- Candles will burn longer on your dining table if you keep them in the freezer for a day until just before you light them.

- Shop when you're not hungry so that your common sense and not your appetite will do the buying; leave the kids at home to avoid the "mommy-I-want-this" hassle; don't take along anyone who doesn't know better than to give in to expensive impulses; most of all, shop from a carefully prepared list.

- Save energy by parboiling potatoes for 5 minutes before baking them. Cuts down oven time considerably. Better yet, do them in a pressure cooker for 10 minutes, then just crisp the skins in the oven for a few minutes.

- Here's a vitamin-saver, too. Steam potatoes for mashing in as little water as possible (a pressure cooker is best for this) so that you end up with very little water. Don't drain the potatoes! Then add instant nonfat dry milk and butter and whip. The cooking water, which is filled with vitamins, plus the powdered milk and butter do the job. Experiment until you get the amounts right.

- Need a new cooking thermometer? Here's the way to tell if you do. Sometime when cooking water is boiling, stick the thermometer into it. It should read 212 degrees, the temperature at which water boils.

- Buy grating cheese (Romano, Parmesan) in a chunk and grind it yourself in a blender or food processor. You save the price of a jar, a label, and labor.

- You can recondition old rusty cast-iron pans with soap and water, followed by steel wool, followed by more soap and water. Dry, rub with vegetable oil, and heat gently.

- To skim the cream from regular, old-fashioned milk, siphon the milk from the bottom, using a nontoxic plastic tube. The cream will slowly sink. When all of the milk is siphoned off, the cream can just be poured into another container.

- Store unpeeled bananas in sealed, wide-mouth jars in the refrigerator and they'll keep a lot longer.

- Eggs will stay fresher longer if stored in the refrigerator with the *small* end of the egg down. This keeps the yolk suspended in the albumen and prevents it from pressing on the lining of the shell, a cause of spoilage.

- Have your own health food store at home. Buy rice, nuts, grains, beans, raisins and other items in generous quantities and store the extras in clean quart jars. Decorate the lids for an attractive display.

- To heat leftover casseroles without turning on the oven, just sit the casserole dish in a larger pan partly filled with water and heat on top of the stove. Keep the casserole covered.

- Turn off your dishwasher before it goes into the automatic-dry cycle and open the door. The air will do the job at absolutely no cost.

- If you don't have a frost-free freezer, use your hair dryer to step up manual defrosting. Be careful not to get a shock.

TIME-SAVERS

- If you have problems with a mixing bowl or cutting board that slips around on the work table, just set it on a damp cloth. It will stay in place. Also, if you're working on waxed paper, dampen the surface of the table a little first, and the paper won't curl up or slip around.

- Take a loaf of your homemade French bread, slice it almost through, cover each slice with melted butter, sprinkle with garlic powder, wrap in foil, and freeze. When company drops in, you'll have garlic bread all ready to heat and serve.

- If you love fresh corn but hate to clean off the silk, just try wiping it with a moistened paper towel. It works.

- Keep commonly used items in little shaker jars. Flour, sugar, paprika, garlic powder—these are all things that can join the salt and pepper on your work counter.

- If company is coming and you have food to keep chilled but no extra refrigerator space, use your picnic ice chest. Or if it's winter, use an unheated garage or even a cardboard box set outdoors. But do keep perishables cold!

- Let a roast stand for 10 minutes at room temperature, and you'll find it's much easier to carve.

- A small squeeze bottle of corn oil (it will keep much longer at room temperature than other vegetable oils) is a real time-saver when kept handy at your stove.

- If you don't have a food processor, you can still grate cabbage or carrots quickly by placing chunks in a blender and covering with water. Whirl for a moment until the vegetable is the desired texture. Pour out into a sieve held over the sink. Shake to remove all excess water, then empty the grated vegetable into a bowl.

- To find herbs and spices quickly, store the jars on your spice shelf in alphabetical order according to the name of the contents.

SAVING THE DAY

- Prevent casseroles or pies from bubbling all over the bottom of your oven by putting a cookie sheet or piece of aluminum foil on the shelf below.

- If you have a grease fire in a pan, use salt. Lots of salt. Salt won't burn—flour will, sugar will—but it will douse the fire quickly. Of course, it will probably ruin the food as well, but so would the fire.

- Prevent burns by turning pot and pan handles so that they don't extend over the edge of the stove.

- If you get a burn, punch a hole in a vitamin E capsule and apply the oil at once. It works.

- For an insect bite, mix a little papaya enzyme—that's in every meat tenderizer and in papaya digestive tablets—with a little hand cream and apply as an ointment. Takes the sting right out.

- Your child has a splinter and you're busy in the kitchen? Try putting a piece of adhesive tape or the sticky tab of a Band-Aid on it, then peeling it off. Frequently it will pull the splinter out easily and painlessly.

- Keep flammables, such as towels and potholders, well away from the range.

- If you have a dripping faucet and a slow plumber, put a sponge under it until he gets there. Catching the drips this way will prevent discoloration of the sink and save you time from scrubbing after the washer is replaced.

- Have an emergency repair kit in the kitchen. A small hammer, a screwdriver, pliers, PVC tape, and assorted nails and hooks. Amazing how many steps they'll save you!
- If you put a square of plastic wrap over the bottom of each glass before stacking it inside another, you'll never have glasses that stick together.

THE MAGIC INGREDIENT

In making your own food, the biggest secret is the same as it is for anything that's worth doing. And that is *wanting to*—wanting healthful, convenient, delicious foods for yourself and your family badly enough to take the trouble to break away from the hypnotic lure of the big food companies' advertising; wanting to badly enough to literally learn a new life-style.

Make your own food. You'll find it's a rewarding experience. The magic ingredient is you.

Index

additives, food, xi–xiv, 1–2
  baby food nutrition and, 156–57
  on fruits and vegetables, 100
  and function, 3
  GRAS, xii
  as industry, xi–xiv
  in luncheon meats, 71
  in meats, 84–86
  poultry raising and, 85
  safety and, 3–5
  in snack items, 172–73
  testing, xii–xiii
  See also cancer; ingredients and
    natural "additives"
alfalfa sprouts, 106–107
  dressing for, 137
Allied Chemicals, xii
almonds, string beans with, 102
American cheese, 65, 68
amino acids, 122
  essential, 122
apple wine, 194
Arabic flat bread, 34
Aspergillus flavus (mold), 4
assisters
  ground-beef, 115–18
  tuna, 118–20
  See also extended foods

baby foods, 156–60
  don'ts, 159

feeding kids and older kids, 160
fruit pasha, 158
fruits, 159
meats, pureed, 159
tips on making, 157–58
vegetables, 159
yogurt, 158
bacon, substitute for, 76
bacteria, food and, 161–62
bagels, 38
  food processor technique for, 39
baking powder, 22–23, 221
bananas
  frozen, as snack, 146
  storing, 224
barbecue
  burger, 91
  chicken, tamari, 91
bars, candy
  carob, 142
  lion's milk, 143
beans, string, almondine, 102
beef
  coating for, 96
  rice and, 118
  scrapple, old-fashioned, 94
  seasoned rice for, 112
  vegetable-beef soup, 79
  See also hamburger meat
beverages, 181–97
  breakfast drinks, 190–92

Mock sour cream

1 c. low-fat cottage cheese
2 tsp. skim milk
2 tsp. lemon juice
Blend in blender

Quiche custard - 2 c. milk or cream
3 whole eggs

Substitute vermouth for dry white wine

3 level Tbsp cocoa + 1 Tbsp. oil or shortening = 1 oz square chocolate